The DREAM MACHINE

MACHINE

EXPLORING THE COMPUTER AGE

Acknowledgements

This book has been written to accompany the television series *The Dream Machine* and is founded on the extensive research which the production teams at the BBC in London and WGBH Television in Boston have carried out. We should like to express our gratitude to Patricia Greenland, Alison Woolnough, Andrew Thompson, Nancy Englander, Rona Remal, Angela Kelley, Lauren Seeley and David Marvit. A special acknowledgment must be made to producers Fiona Homes, Nancy Linde and Bob Hone, whose finely crafted programmes provided the basis for much of the material. We should also like to thank Paul E Ceruzzi, Martin Campbell-Kelly and Hubert Dreyfus for helpful comments on the manuscript.

Note to readers

All uncited quotations are from interviews carried out for the television series.

PICTURE CREDITS

Every effort has been made to trace the copyright owners of the photographs reproduced. We apologize to anyone whose copyright we have unwittingly infringed

Key to abbreviations: a = above b = below   c = centre   l = left r = right

SPL = Science Photo Library

(Black and white photographs listed by page no.)
13 (*c*) Science Museum; 13 (*l*) BBC/photo Derrick Witty; 13 (*r*) Science Museum; 15 BBC; 16–23 Science Museum; 24 IBM; 25–7 Science Museum; 32 Konrad Zuse; 35 (*l*) Konrad Zuse; 36 Mullard Ltd; 38 Tommy Flowers; 40 Crown Copyright; 40 Courtesy of Hagley Museum and Library; 41 Crown Copyright; 42 (*b*) Imperial War Museum; 43 Kay Mauchly-Antonelli (*top*); 43 (*b*) Dept of the Army, Washington (*middle*); 44 MIT Museum (*bottom*); 45 IBM; 50 Science Museum; 55 National Physical Laboratory; 61 The Hulton-Deutsch Collection; 62 ICL; 64 General Instrument; 65 (*a*) J. Lyons; 65 (*b*) Hulton/Deutsch; 66–7 Harry Wulforst; 70–73 IBM; 79 British Film Institute; 80–3 IBM; 85 Mullard; 87–8 National Semiconductor; 89 Wayne Miller/Magnum; 92–3 SPL; 92 (*b*) Science Museum; 93 MIT; 96 Haruko/Digital; 99 Doug Engelbart; 102 Xerox Corporation; 107 Intel; 100–113 John Calhoun; 115 Sally and Richard Greenhill; 116 Cindy Charles/Gamma/Frank Spooner Pictures; 117 Frank Spooner Pictures; 122 Apple; 128 Sally and Richard Greenhill; 129 Michael Holford; 130 (*a*) A F Kersting; 130 (*b*) Woodmansterne; 137 MIT; 139–140 Topham Picture Source; 141 NIT; 142 Ann Ronan Picture Library; 143 Dept of Artificial Intelligence, University of Edinburgh; 148–9 Chrisian Vionjard/Gamma/Frank Spooner Pictures; 174 Patrick Piel/Gamma/Frank Spooner Pictures

COLOUR SECTIONS
(Colour pictures listed by picture no.)
Ann Ronan Picture Library *photo* 19; Apple *photos* 13 & 14; Gamma *photo* 12; Kermaniliaison *photo* 16; NCA *photo* 10; Science Museum *photos* 8 (CRNI), 15, 17 & 18 (Peter Menzel), 21 (David Parker), 9 (Alfred Pasienka) and 20 (Jorge Sclar).

The DREAM MACHINE

EXPLORING THE COMPUTER AGE

Jon Palfreman & Doron Swade

BBC BOOKS

Published by BBC Books
a division of BBC Enterprises Limited
Woodlands, 80 Wood Lane, London W12 0TT

First published 1991
© Jon Palfreman and Doron Swade 1991

ISBN 0 563 36221 9

Designed by Grahame Dudley Associates

Illustrations by Grahame Dudley Associates

Set in 11/18 pt Bodoni by
Butler & Tanner Ltd, Frome, Somerset

Printed and bound in Great Britain
by Butler & Tanner Ltd, Frome, Somerset

Colour separations by Dot Gradations Ltd, Chelmsford

Jacket printed by Lawrence Allen Ltd, Weston-super-Mare

C ontents

*I*ntroduction

It is a source of bemusement to many that the word 'computer' could ever have meant anything other than a machine. Yet this use of the word is relatively recent. The 'computers' referred to in the nineteenth century by Charles Babbage, the great British ancestral figure in the history of computing, were not machines but people who performed calculations. And as late as 1936 Alan Turing, a pioneer of electronic computing, also referred to people as 'computers'.[1] There are accounts of people being described as computers as late as the 1950s. But by that time, when most people spoke of computers they were talking about a new machine – the electronic digital computer.

The first electronic computers emerged from engineers' laboratories some 40 years ago. They were rare, ponderous and expensive behemoths with capabilities that now seem startlingly trivial. Less than 15 years ago computers were catapulted into our personal lives with the advent of affordable mass-produced computers. The personal computer boom of the early 1980s gave immediacy to a phenomenon about which much had been said but which had remained, for most of us, a remote and possibly sinister part of the industrial, commercial and military establishments. Personal computers gave individuals a sense of involvement in what is seen by many as one of the most remarkable phenomena of our age.

But it was not until those personal computers had enough power to carry out the elaborate programs ('software') available in the second half of the 1980s, that computers began to signal their future. Desk-top machines which could execute 2 million instructions a second made possible a critical change not only in what computers could do, but in how they were perceived. No longer did computers have to be difficult to use, no longer was their use confined to problems involving numbers. With suitable software the computer could become everyone's dream machine.

Sophisticated software, running on powerful computers, could offer the user an illusion, on screen, of a world they understood – an illusion of a desk top with files, a keyboard with notes, an architect's drawing board.

Any new technology is difficult to interpret. Typically, it tends to be defined in terms of the technology it replaced or the problem it solved. The car was initially called 'the horseless carriage', and the radio 'the wireless'. Of all our technologies the computer has been the hardest to interpret because it is a fundamentally different kind of machine. During its 40-year history, predictions about its future have often proved to be wildly inaccurate.

Computers were invented to do arithmetic, and for years most computer scientists thought of them only in this way. The builders of the first stored program computers after the Second World War could foresee, for the most part, only a few scientific and military applications for the new machine. They had little comprehension of how widespread the computer would become or the numerous uses which would be found for it.

7

8

It was commonly believed that only a handful of 'electronic brains' would be needed by any one country. Douglas Hartree, the English mathematician and physicist, is quoted as saying: 'We have a computer here in Cambridge; there is one in Manchester, and one at the NPL [National Physical Laboratory]. I suppose there ought to be one in Scotland, but that's about all.'[2] And in 1947, Howard Aiken, the American mathematician and computer engineer, predicted that only six electronic digital computers would satisfy all the United States' computing needs.[3]

Today, with over 100 million personal computers in the world, these predictions seem laughable. The electronics industry is the third largest in the global economy after automobiles and oil. The turnover of a manufacturer like IBM is comparable to the gross national product (GNP) of some small industrialized nations. But in 1950 the very idea of a commercial computer industry seemed far-fetched, given the awesome cost of the new machines. In today's money, the first electronic computing machine, the ENIAC (Electronic Numerical Integrator and Computer), would cost almost $US 3 million to construct. No one foresaw the phenomenal drop in the price and size of hardware, and the opportunities this would bring. Now, machines with many times the ENIAC's power sell for just a few hundred dollars.

Few people saw the computer's versatility, or imagined that a huge software industry would develop to write programs to suit a staggering array of needs. And the surprises are not over. While computers have revolutionized everything from science to banking, we will argue that their real historical and cultural significance is much greater – something children born in the last half of the 1980s are learning for themselves.

When children begin to recognize their surroundings they note the objects around them and discover their purpose by observing and interacting with them. For children born after 1984, the modern computer, replete with user-friendly software, is just another object in their world along with cars and televisions. Unaware of the computer's past, unaware that it was (and still is) seen by many as a number cruncher, and having no interest in how it works (since apart from the buttons and mouse there are no visible moving parts), these children view the computer differently from the rest of us. Ask a five-year-old what a computer is and he or she will give you answers like 'It's for drawing and making designs ... it helps me to read and write ... it's for playing games.' For young children, it is an object that mediates between them and the things they like to do. It is not really a machine at all, but a personal medium of expression and communication.

We will argue that they are right: the modern computer is more like a book than a machine. In its day, the book had to overcome many of the same obstacles to gain acceptance. While a paperback now sells for less than most people earn in an hour, its medieval ancestor was priceless, and every bit as valuable as an early mainframe computer in the 1950s. Like the book, the computer has become smaller, lighter and cheaper and we can carry some models with us.

There the similarities end. Unlike the book, a computer is dynamic. It can change its own markings. Unlike a book, a computer can *process* information, simulating other media from text to television. A computer can communicate with other computers throughout the world enabling the emergence of new kinds of electronic communities and patterns of social behaviour. Also, the computer is capable of making the user feel he is inside a three-dimensional space (say a building) in which he can move, and which he can experience as if it were real – so-called virtual realities. (We discuss these in detail in Chapter 6.) We are seeing only the first signs that computers are rooting themselves in our culture. Whereas it took the written word thousands of years to become the cornerstone of our intellectual and commercial lives, computers have been around for only four decades.

The computer started as a machine to manipulate numbers. It was invented to do fast and accurately the kind of arithmetic humans usually do slowly and inaccurately. But a few perceptive people, like the British

9

10

mathematician Alan Turing, realized that arithmetic was only one example of the kind of mental process that could be carried out 'mechanically'. For Turing, 'computing' was a logical rather than a numerical process. It followed that a 'computing machine' could be thought of as a general device for manipulating symbols which could represent anything we chose.

With the advent of electronic computers, issues in logic and perception, which had occupied philosophers for centuries, acquired a new immediacy. Attempts by artificial intelligence researchers to write programs to model human thought and intelligence have illuminated our understanding of these elusive and perplexing concepts. The failures have been as instructive and surprising as the successes. What has been regarded as exceptional talent in a person has often proved a commonplace accomplishment for a computer. In the nineteenth century, an English school teacher called William Shanks, devoted 28 years of his life to calculate the decimal expansion of π (Pi) to 707 places. It was later discovered that he made a mistake at the 528th place.

Today, a program called Mathematica will, if you type in 'N (Pi, 707)', calculate the answer in seven seconds. The same program can solve many problems on a first year university calculus exam.

On the other hand, acts which are easy for us to perform – like telling a dog from a cat, walking through a room of furniture, recognizing a friend, reading handwriting, and understanding speech – have proved profoundly difficult to model on computers. Computers are the *idiot savants* of the twentieth century. They are devices with remarkable specific abilities but are woefully feeble-minded the rest of the time. Our attitude to them is often a curious combination of wariness and wonder. But even this may be about to change.

It is hard to interpret a revolution when you are in the midst of one, but this book is an attempt to do just that. It is a story of the rise of a new technology and the remarkable people behind it; the story of how an exotic and fabulously expensive machine evolved into a small desk-top device and began anchoring itself in our culture. It is in some ways a tragic story, for at every stage there were those who saw the computer's enormous possibilities. Such visionaries, from Babbage to Doug Engelbart, a young American engineer, were generally unable to convince their colleagues, and their work often had little discernible influence on the subsequent development of the technology. Only later was their great insight appreciated and their place in history recognized.

The tale starts from the earliest attempts to represent numbers and mechanize calculation. From these modest beginnings emerged a dream of a general-purpose machine unlike anything the world had yet seen.

11

*C*omputing

before there were computers

'One evening I was sitting in the rooms of the Analytical Society at Cambridge [University], my head leaning forward on the Table in a kind of dreamy mood, with a Table of logarithms lying open before me. Another member, coming into the room, and seeing me half asleep, called out, "Well, Babbage, what are you dreaming about?" to which I replied, "I am thinking that all these Tables [pointing to the logarithms] might be calculated by machinery."' [1]

For thousands of years physical aids have helped people count and do arithmetic. Loose counters, pebbles, and tokens of various kinds were used to keep track of calculations mainly for accounting and trade. The word 'calculus' is Latin for pebble. An elementary form of mechanization is found in the wire-and-bead abacus – a rectangular, usually wooden, frame with beads strung on wires or dowels thought to date from the Middle Ages. The position of the bead indicates its value and the user moves the beads according to certain rules in order to perform calculations.

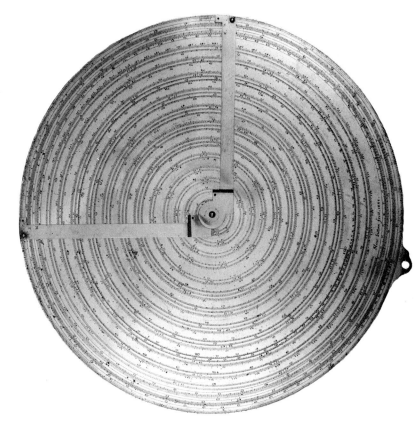

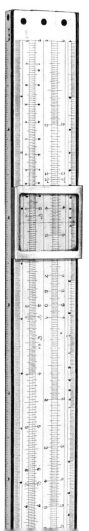

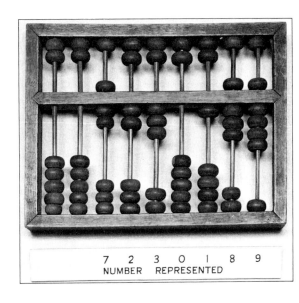

7 2 3 0 1 8 9
NUMBER REPRESENTED

Bottom left: Chinese abacus. Upper beads represent '5's, lower beads, '1's. The number represented is 7,230,189.

Far left: Slide rule. In widespread use until the 1970s.

Above: Spiral slide rule by Henry Sutton, 1663.

The mechanization of calculation

The first documented efforts to build *automatic* calculating machines date from the seventeenth century. The aim was to produce a device not only to represent the states of the numbers themselves (like the abacus) but also to carry out arithmetical procedures like adding and multiplication. There were notable attempts by the German academic Wilhelm Schickard, the French mathematician Blaise Pascal, and Gottfried Wilhelm Leibniz, the German mathematician and philosopher, to make working models of mechanical calculators. But the models were neither reliable nor automatic. They were particularly afflicted by the 'carry problem' – the physical difficulty of getting the number 9 in a display of numbers to trigger the carrying of a 1 to the next column in an addition problem. Not until the nineteenth century was a calculating machine designed that solved these problems.

The mainstay of human calculators was the mathematical table, published on a large scale from the late eighteenth century. These tables contained a vast range of calculations, from multiplications and divisions to logarithms. Mathematicians, scientists, astronomers, navigators, engineers and actuaries relied on them for all but the simplest calculations. The problem was that the tables were riddled with errors – errors of calculation, errors of transcription and errors in printing. The first edition of the *Nautical Ephemeris for Finding Latitude and Longitude at Sea* was found by one seaman to contain over 1000 mistakes.

The accuracy problem was of great concern to Charles Babbage, a brilliant polymath and mathematician. Babbage was an expert on calculation tables and his own collection contained about 300 volumes of them. During a particularly grim session checking tables commissioned by the Astronomical Society, Babbage turned to his friend John Herschel, the astronomer, and said: 'I wish to God

14

Gr	20		†			
20 mi.	Sinus	Logarithmi	Differentia	Logarithmi	Sinus	
0	3420201	10728852	10106827	622025	9396926	60
1	3422934	10720865	10097781	623084	9395931	59
2	3425667	10712885	10088741	624144	9394935	58
3	3428400	10704912	10079707	625205	9393938	57
4	3431133	10696945	10070678	626167	9392940	56
5	3433865	10688984	10061654	627330	9391941	55
6	3436597	10681030	10052636	628394	9390942	54
7	3439329	10673085	10043616	629459	6389942	53
8	3442060	10665147	10034822	630525	9388941	52
9	3444791	10657216	10025624	631592	9387939	51
10	3447522	10649292	10016632	632660	9386937	50
11	3450253	10641375	10007646	633729	9385934	49
12	3452983	10633465	9998666	634799	9384930	48
13	3455713	10625562	9989692	635870	9383925	47
14	3458442	10617667	9980725	636942	9382919	46
15	3461171	10609772	9271764	638015	9381913	45
16	3463900	10601898	9962810	639088	9380906	44
17	3466629	10594024	9953862	640162	9379898	43
18	3469357	10586157	9944920	641237	9378889	42
19	3472085	10578297	9935984	642313	9377880	41
20	3474813	10570444	9927054	643390	9376870	40
21	3477540	10562598	9918130	644468	9375859	39
22	3480267	10554760	9909213	645547	9374847	38
23	3482994	10546929	9900302	646627	9373834	37
24	3485721	10539104	9891396	647708	9372820	36
25	3488447	10531286	9882496	648790	9371806	35
26	3491173	10523474	9873601	649873	9370791	34
27	3493899	10515669	9864711	650958	9369775	33
28	3496624	10507871	9855827	652044	9368758	32
29	3499343	10500080	9846949	653131	9367740	31
30	3502075	10492295	9838076	654219	9366722	30

Page of logarithm tables by John Napier, 1620.

these calculations had been executed by steam.'[2]

That was in 1821. During the next 10 years Babbage designed and developed a monumentally ambitious machine called the Difference Engine, the first complete design for an automatic calculating device. With it, he sought to eliminate humans from the calculating process, solve the 'carry problem' and make the printing of tables integral to the machine.[3]

But for a variety of technical, political and financial reasons the Difference Engine was never built. Following a dispute with his engineer, persistent financial difficulties, and little to show after a decade of development, work stopped and was not resumed. The machine that would have weighed several tons and consisted of an estimated 25 000 parts was not to be.[4]

In 1832, however, a small section, about one-seventh of the full size machine, was assembled and demonstrated. This partial assembly is regarded as the first automatic calculator and still works to this day.[5]

Within a few years of reading a description of Babbage's efforts, published in 1834, Georg and Edvard Scheutz, a Swedish father and son team, were inspired to construct their own difference engine. They built three machines, all of which worked after a fashion. To the Scheutzes go the honour of completing the first printing difference engine and producing the first tables automatically calculated and printed by machinery.

16

Edvard Scheutz, late 1850s.

Charles Babbage, in 1860 at nearly 70 years old.

17

The analytical engine

But to Babbage goes a greater honour. For in the midst of his distress over failing to build his Difference Engine he conceived of a fundamentally new kind of machine which he called the Analytical Engine. It is for this second machine that he is principally remembered today.

Babbage's Difference Engine, like the earlier Schickard, Pascal and Leibniz calculators, was designed to perform a fixed and limited set of arithmetic operations, mainly additions and subtractions. By contrast, the Analytical Engine was designed as a programmable general-purpose machine for finding the value of virtually any algebraic equation. It shared many features with modern electronic computers, and today ranks as one of the most startling intellectual achievements of the nineteenth century.

Babbage's Difference Engine computed and printed a range of mathematical tables using a single computational technique called the method of differences. Like the machines of the Industrial Revolution, the Difference Engine was a special-purpose machine. Throughout history, a machine has been defined in terms of the particular function it carries out. A machine *is* what a machine *does*. A train is a machine which transports people and things, a printing press is a device which prints

Design drawing for part of the Analytical Engine, 1841.

18

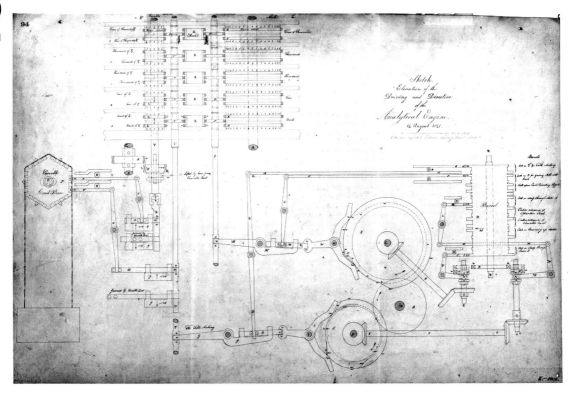

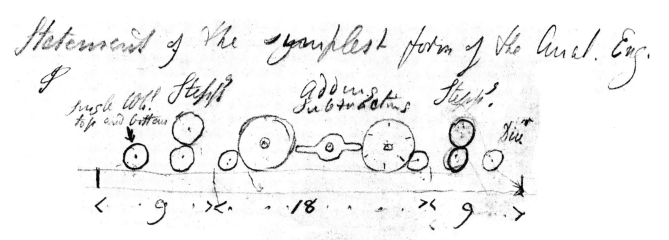

Babbage's sketch for the
simplified mill of the
Analytical Engine, 1870.

19

letters and images on paper. Such a definition of a machine was fine when machines were intended for physical tasks, but in the realm of thought it soon becomes a rigid constraint. The mind is notable for its general-purpose intellectual abilities – it can compute using the method of differences, but it can also handle other arithmetic procedures and can, in addition, compose a sonnet or imagine a picture. Any special-purpose mental machine like the Difference Engine was destined to seem very limited compared with the tasks that the mind could dream up for such mental machines to do. Charles

Babbage was led to a grander conception of a machine with general-purpose capabilities, a machine which he called his Analytical Engine. Unlike other machines the Analytical Engine would not be built to carry out a specific calculation like the method of differences, rather it would be designed with the ability to follow orders to carry out many kinds of calculation. It would, in modern parlance, be programmable.

Using imagery from the textile industry, Babbage called the machinery which performed the calculations the 'mill' and the columns of cogwheels representing numbers, the 'store'. The separation of 'store' and 'mill' (or memory and central processor) is a fundamental feature of the internal organization of modern computers and it is remarkable that pioneers of electronic computers ended up with the same arrangement, apparently without any detailed knowledge of Babbage's designs. Most importantly, the machine was programmable and Babbage stored the strings of instructions on punched cards.

The punched cards technique originated from the Jacquard loom which used such cards to control the patterns woven with thread. Drawing on the analogy, Ada Lovelace, a talented amateur mathematician and confidante of Babbage, wrote that it 'weaves algebraic patterns just as the Jacquard loom weaves flowers and leaves'.

Babbage first conceived of the Analytical Engine shortly after the Difference Engine had come to its bleak end in 1833. By 1840 he had produced a basic design. The Analytical Engine dwarfed even the Difference Engine. The 1840s scheme, had it been built, would have been the size of a small locomotive. Not only was it not built, there was no single definitive design but a progression of designs that Babbage developed and refined over nearly half a century.

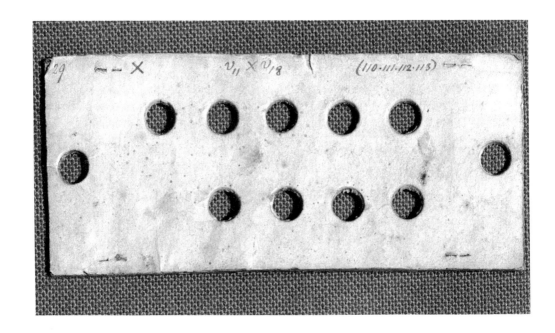

Left: Punched 'Operation
card' for Babbage's
Analytical Engine.

Above: Jacquard loom. The
pattern of the weave is
controlled by punched cards.

21

Demoralized by the psychological and financial cost of the unsuccessful Difference Engine project, Babbage made no concerted attempt to raise funds to build a full-scale Analytical Engine. At the time of his death in 1871 a simplified version of the engine's mill was under construction. After Babbage's death, his son, Henry P Babbage, built a large hand-operated calculator with a printer which was based on the design of the mill. This was completed in 1910 and used to calculate and print (not without difficulty) the first 23 multiples of π to 29 decimal places. This sole remaining part of the Analytical Engine together with the Difference Engine assembly are the great icons in the prehistory of computing.

Commercial machines

While the quest for general-purpose automatic computation ended with Babbage's death, the building of calculating machines did not. Thomas de Colmar, a French businessman, had produced the first successful commercial calculator in the early 1820s. His 'arithmometer' was capable of the four basic arithmetic functions. It was not automatic, but manually operated and the user had to be informed to some extent about what he was doing. But unlike its predecessors, the device was reliable and by the end of the century, de Colmar-type arithmometers had a sizeable following and such desk-top calculators were steadily improved.

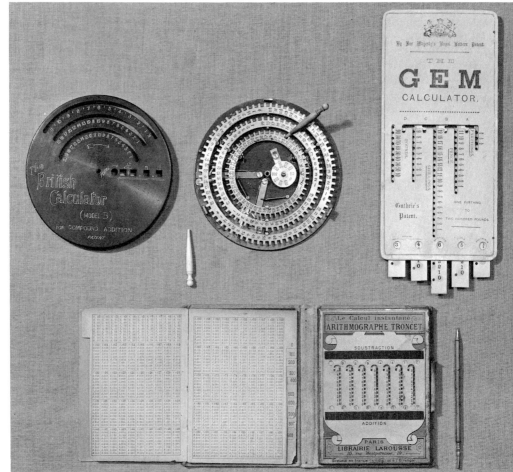

Three portable mechanical aids to calculation. Top left: 'Brical' calculator, patented 1905. Top right: 'GEM' calculator. Bottom: Troncet's 'arithmograph', c1889.

Data processing was the second class of mental task to be mechanized, and a new office-machine industry emerged in the late nineteenth century. The problem was one of information management rather than calculation. The US Census Bureau in the 1880s was in an information management crisis. Data from the 1880 census had taken over seven years to analyze.[6] The process was almost entirely manual with scores of clerks required to count and classify information from millions of record sheets. With the huge influx of immigrants into the United States the Census Bureau faced the prospect of failing to process all the data from the 1890 census before the 1900 census was due.

Herman Hollerith, a newly graduated engineer from Columbia University in New York City, devised an electric tabulating system which revolutionized data processing. Data from the census was coded on punched

23

Key-driven desk top calculator called a 'comptograph'.

Herman Hollerith

24

cards using a specially designed card punch. Each of the categories of information – age, sex, marital status etc – was represented by specific holes on a small area of the card. Hollerith built an electrical 'pin press' to detect whether a hole was covered. When the hand-operated press was closed a large cluster of sprung pins would press on the card. Where holes had been punched, the pins would pass through and dip into a mercury cup to close an electrical circuit. Counters connected to each of these circuits accumulated total numbers of individuals in the various categories. With a tabulator, a census clerk could process more than

7000 cards a day, though the record for a single day was nearly three times this number.

Hollerith's tabulating system was readily adopted for the United States census and soon after in Europe. The versatility of the system created the demand for more sophisticated analyses. The punched card system of managing and analyzing large quantities of information found enthusiastic users in accounting, banking and industry. Punched-card machines became the mainstay of the office-machine and data processing industries and dominated automated information management for well over half a century until electronic computers became affordable stand-alone products in the late 1950s. Hollerith's Tabulating Machine Company, founded in 1896, ultimately evolved, with three other companies, into IBM. On the other side of the Atlantic, the British Tabulating Machine Company, founded in 1907, would later become known as ICL.

By the 1930s, the point at which we arrive at the birth of electronic computing, we find two thriving industries: a calculator industry

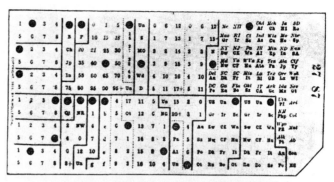

Industrial population Census Card covering the Twelfth U. S. Census, compiled in 1900.

Above: Cover of the Scientific American of 30 August 1890 featuring Hollerith's system.

Top right: Punched card for the 1900 US census.

Middle right: Hollerith vertical sorter and counter, c1910.

Bottom: BTM tabulator production, May 1949.

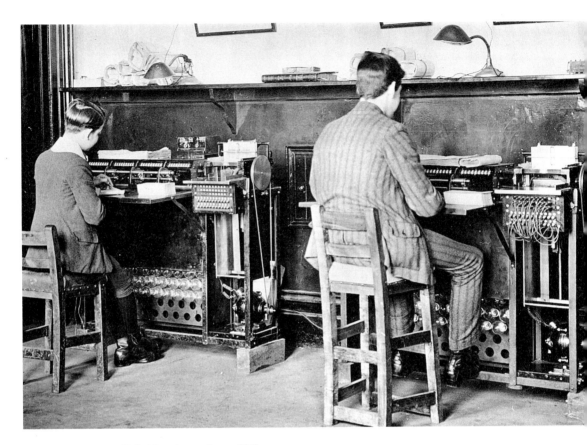

Above: Hollerith equipment in use c1910.

making manual desk-top calculators for numerical calculation and an office-machine industry making semi-automatic punched-card equipment for data processing.

In contrast, Babbage's dream of a general-purpose automatic computing machine had all but been abandoned. Yet in the next decade, under the stimulus of the Second World War, the dream would be revived and successfully implemented in working hardware. The success of the first giant computers would lead to the creation of a computer industry which would subsume the data processing industry and much of the calculator industry too.

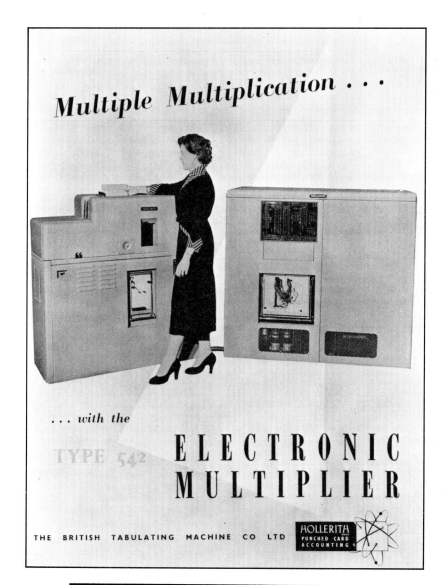

Multiple Multiplication . . .

. . . with the

TYPE 542

ELECTRONIC MULTIPLIER

THE BRITISH TABULATING MACHINE CO LTD

HOLLERITH
PUNCHED CARD
ACCOUNTING

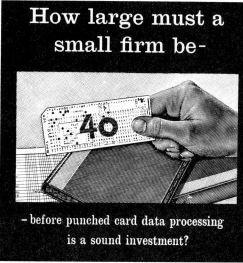

How large must a small firm be-

– before punched card data processing is a sound investment?

Above: Advertisement for Hollerith BTM Electronic Multiplier. First version was introduced in the early 1950s.

Near left: Part of an advertisement for automatic office equipment by International Computers and Tabulators Ltd (ICT), c1960.

CHAPTER 2

*T*he birth

of electronic computing

Babbage had seen that to be truly useful, a calculating machine should be capable of not just one function but any that might be required. While Babbage was mainly thinking of arithmetic operations, there is some evidence that he glimpsed that more was at stake. In future years, brilliant philosophers and mathematicians like Fredrich Frege, Bertrand Russell, Alfred North Whitehead and Kurt Gödel, the Austrian-born logician, would demonstrate that arithmetic is only one example of human reasoning and that underlying arithmetic is something more fundamental – logic.

It followed that other mental procedures (code breaking, solving puzzles and playing chess) could, if cast in precise logical terms, be mechanized. During the eighteenth and nineteenth centuries logic machines did appear which proved that traditional syllogisms could be solved on a machine. But the radical implications of this were not fully appreciated until 1936 when a young mathematician called Alan Turing wrote a paper on mathematical logic, approaching computing machines from a novel direction.

Turing was not interested in building automatic computing machines and may not even have known much about Charles Babbage.

He was, however, interested in the concept of computability. His interest had been focused by his teacher, Max Newman, a Cambridge mathematician, who had given a lecture series dealing with the latest discoveries in mathematical logic including those of Kurt Gödel. One large if arcane question which Gödel had not resolved was whether there was a definite method, 'a mechanical process', that could be applied to a mathematical statement and that would decide whether that statement was provable?

The words 'mechanical process' started Turing thinking about machines. Could a machine be designed, he wondered, which could in principle compute all mathematical statements? While he had no intention of building it, Turing hoped that thinking about such a machine would help him to formulate a rigorous definition of computing – how by following a definite process, a solution to a problem is computed. The computers of Turing's time were still people rather than machines. These computers worked with pencil and paper, following instructions (which told them how to do the calculation),

29

Left: Alan Turing

30

reading numbers (which they needed for the input), processing them (mentally or with a hand calculator) and writing down new numbers (the intermediate results). Turing tried to abstract the essentials of this process by imagining a machine that could do the same thing as the human computer mechanically. The essential process is that numbers were transformed into other numbers using rules. The machine consisted only of a scanner and a long tape. The scanner could move up and down the tape and read, write and erase symbols on the tape. The symbols on the tape (say numbers) were manipulated according to rules of transition which were physically embodied inside the machine. As such, this Turing machine was a classical machine like the Difference Engine. But Turing realized that there was no reason why these instructions (the rules) had to be built into the 'hardware' of his imaginary machine. They were after all just rules. They could be put on the front of the same tape that held the numbers. Now the actual machine could be even simpler. All it had to be able to do was follow instructions that would give it the

rules about how to transform one symbol into another.

This was not a machine in the classical sense. Like Babbage's Analytical Engine it too had more than one specific function. Its only purpose – the only thing the hardware had to do – was follow orders. Only when it read these instructions on the tape would it know what to do, and what machine to be. Each new tape with new orders and new numbers changed it into a different machine. *One* computing machine could therefore perform the task of *any* computing machine. In principle, his imaginary machine could compute anything a human computer could compute, given enough tape and time. Because of its universal qualities of simulating all other machines, this imaginary machine became later known as a Universal Turing Machine.

Using the thought-device of a Universal Turing machine, Turing was able to resolve the somewhat esoteric issue he had set out to solve: that there would always be problems which could not be computed (problems for which the theoretical Turing machine would never halt) and these problems could not be predicted. But this achievement is now just a small footnote in history.

Alan Turing proved there was no machine that could solve all mathematical problems, but in doing so conceived of something far more important – that there was a universal machine which could simulate any other machine, simply by reading the tapes that described them. Turing's fame comes from the remarkable twist that he gave a definition of a computer, *before one was actually built.* He had shown that it was theoretically, logically and mathematically possible to build a computing machine which could automatically carry out any set of instructions which could be computed in a finite time – anything, in short, that a human computer could do. But Turing went further. Being a logician, he knew that there was nothing special about numbers. Numbers were symbols, but there were other kind of symbols; letters for example. If one kind of symbol could be manipulated by a Universal Turing Machine then any symbol could be manipulated provided that one knew the rules the machine had to follow.

Given the right set of instructions, the Universal Turing Machine could for instance, take the letters of Alan Turing's name and find all the three-letter words in the *Oxford English Dictionary* using only those letters (assuming the dictionary was also supplied on the tape). It might also in principle play a game of chess.

Donald Michie, a British academic, who later worked with Turing, puts it like this: 'The significance to mathematical logicians was obvious. At the same time it raised a very definite practical question mark. Namely, could this logical construction of the Universal Turing Machine actually be embodied in hardware?' In 1945, less than 10 years later, Turing wrote a draft report on the prospects for building a full-scale model of a new machine – the electronic embodiment of a Turing Machine – better known as the digital computer.

Pioneers of a new machine

The years between Turing's paper on compatibility and his 1945 Report subtitled 'Proposed

31

Electronic Calculator' are among the most fascinating and muddled in the history of computing. The idea of building automatic calculating machines was back in vogue: commercial calculating machines in the 1930s, arithmometers and comptometers, could not do large calculations automatically, of the kind that engineers and scientists increasingly needed. So experts in Germany, Britain and the United States were again motivated to study the problem of automating number crunching.

Germany

The story starts in Germany with Konrad Zuse. If circumstances had been different, the first digital electronic computer might well have been built there. By 1936, the year of Turing's paper, Zuse, a young engineer, was hard at work in his parents' living room building automatic computing machines. As a civil engineering student Zuse hated having to solve tedious and difficult calculations, and would later muse: 'You could say that I was too lazy to calculate so I invented the computer.'[1]

32

Right: Konrad Zuse with the Z4.

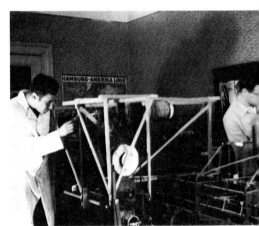

Above: Konrad Zuse (right) and Helmut Schreyer (left) working on the Z1.
Left: The Z1 in the living room of Zuse's parents' home.

What is startling about Zuse's work is that he knew almost nothing of what had gone before. He had not heard of Babbage[2], and knew nothing of the workings of mechanical analog machines[3] or punched-card machines. Zuse started from scratch.

Zuse built his machine differently from all other machines. Traditionally a machine is built up of complex subsections. An airplane, for example, has several sections including a tail section, wings and engines. Such a design makes it very good for flying but means that it is rather difficult to transform it into a car or a washing machine. A truly general-purpose machine, however, had to be able to transform itself to carry out many different functions. What is striking is that a human computer, using very few elements (a few numbers, some procedures like adding and subtracting and some rules) is able to do almost any kind of arithmetic problem. Zuse reasoned that a computing machine made up of very simple elements which could be harnessed to do different things offered the best approach. And to an engineer the simplest element is one which can

assume only one of two states – a switch. This in turn led him to use the binary system.

Virtually all calculators up to that time had mimicked our use of ten counting digits. Probably because we have ten fingers, almost all human societies count in tens. It is so ingrained, it seems to be the only natural way for humans to count. But what is easy for humans is not necessarily easy for machines. The problem of designing calculators which could handle the ten numbers (including such manoeuvres as adding 1 to 999999 and having the carries ripple through the digits) had plagued calculator builders since Schickard. There is nothing sacred about counting in tens however; there are many possible ways of counting. The simplest number system is the binary number system which has only two numbers '1' and '0'. In a binary system the machine only has to distinguish between two possible states. The advantage of the system to Zuse was that the value of a binary digit (a 'bit') can be represented by one of only two positions of a mechanical or electrical part. The mechanical part repre-

33

34

senting a bit is, in effect, a switch which is either on or off.

Anything which can be counted in tens can be counted in binary. For example the number 335 in decimal is composed of three 'hundreds', three 'tens', and five 'units'. In binary that same number is somewhat longer 101001111 (going from right to left: one 'one', one 'two', one 'four', one 'eight', no 'sixteen', no 'thirty two', one 'sixty four', no 'one hundred and twenty eight', one 'two hundred and fifty six'). The binary system uses more bits, and therefore more individual moving parts, to represent the value of a given number than does the decimal system. But this loss of physical economy is more than made up for by the greater simplicity of the machine's mechanism.

Zuse's second crucial decision was to build a machine in which information was passed through logic gates instead of adding wheels. Logic gates were particular arrangements of switches which could modify and combine binary digits (0s and 1s). With a combination of logic gates one can carry out any task in arithmetic. Two binary numbers passing through

one set of logic gates will be added, the same pair of numbers passing through a second set of gates will be subtracted and so on.

Conceptually, Zuse had already passed beyond the mechanical cog wheel world of Charles Babbage for the advantage of a logic gate construction was that it didn't matter what the logic gates were constructed of. Any technology would do, if it allowed for switching between two states. While Zuse began by using mechanical switches, in the 1930s there were a number of alternatives available. The obvious one for a binary switch was the telephone relay – an electromechanical device which could assume only two states.

Zuse assigned his attempts to build working hardware Z numbers. His Z-1 and Z-2 machines were slow and never worked reliably. The Z-3, however, (which was operational in 1941) used electromechanical relays throughout and has the distinction of being the first fully operational program-controlled calculator. It used some 2 600 relays. To program the machine, he ingeniously got round wartime shortages by using discarded

my workshop and said: "You ought to do this with valves." I thought he was joking at first. But we thought about it, and the idea that you would be able to calculate 1000 times faster was magic.'[4]

Electronic valves (known as vacuum tubes in the United States), were mainly used at that time in radios to detect and amplify weak signals, but it was well known that they could

Left: Konrad Zuse with a reconstruction of his Z1.

Below: A thermionic valve. Known in the United States as a vacuum tube.

movie film with holes punched in it. The arithmetic unit could add, subtract, divide, multiply, find square roots and perform binary-to-decimal conversion and the reverse. But even though it was fast by mechanical standards, practically, it was still too slow, taking about a third of a second for an addition and three to five seconds to multiply two numbers. A new technology was needed to break the speed barrier.

Helmut Schreyer, a friend from Zuse's university days, suggested that such a technology was available. As Zuse recalls: '[Schreyer] came to also be used as switching components. As they were capable of switching extremely quickly, they held the promise of being at least 1000 times faster than the relays used by Zuse in the Z-3. Whereas a relay could only work as fast as a physical object could move, in a valve, switching was done by electrons jumping between the plates millions of times a second. An electronic machine with the logical structure of the Z-3 had the potential to transform the fortunes of automatic calculation and give Germany's scientists and engineers a valuable new tool. Zuse and Schreyer estimated that such a machine would take two years to develop and sought the support they needed to build it.

They did not receive it. They were turned down by the German High Command on the grounds that the Second World War would soon be over. Germany's chance to be first in the race to develop digital electronic computers had vanished. But if Hitler failed to seize this opportunity he was responsible (albeit unknowingly) for promoting the introduction of high speed electronics in other countries – such as Britain.

Hitler's directives to his commanders in the field were sent by teleprinter. To the Allies these were extremely important military messages for they gave a clear indication of the Germans' strategy. But when they were intercepted and sent to Bletchley Park, the isolated Buckinghamshire country house which was the headquarters of the British decoding effort, they presented a nightmarish problem.

England

The security of communications in the Allied and German commands relied on coding messages before transmission and decoding them on receipt. Complex coding machines were used to scramble and unscramble the messages at each end. To unscramble an intercepted message cypher-breakers needed to know the 'key' that had been used to code it. The more complex the code, the more secure the message, and the bigger the headache for the code-crackers.

The security of coded messages was so important that the

Germans developed a number of different coding machines. The well-known German 'Enigma' machines were used by the German Navy for enciphering and deciphering tactical signals. Each letter was entered and changed by the machine into another letter – the coded one – according to the key; the key was the set of rules that translated the plain text letters into coded letters. The same key was obviously needed at the receiving end to make sense of the message. Finding the key was daunting. The German Enigma machine, for example, had three or four rotating wheels, each with up to 26 possible contacts through which to route the circuit connecting the uncoded and coded letter. The position of the rotors changed automatically as the message progressed; the same letter entered twice in succession would usually produce two different results. To cap it all, the Germans kept changing the settings. The upshot was that the number of possible combinations relating two letters ran into thousands of billions.

The German High Command used a machine even more sophisticated than the Enigma. Called

the Lorenz, it was an example of a type of machine called *Geheimschreiber*, 'secret writer'. The staggering task for Allied intelligence and the code-crackers at the Code and Cypher School at Bletchley Park was not only to break the code, but to do so quickly before events overtook the relevance of the information. In late 1942, a new member of staff, the Cambridge University mathematician, Max Newman, arrived at Bletchley. Newman thought it should be possible to automate part of the decoding process. The belief that the codes could be broken by an automatic machine might well have been reinforced by Newman's knowledge of the work of Alan Turing. Newman had been Turing's supervisor at Cambridge and now both of them were working at Bletchley. A machine which reads input symbols – German coded messages – and transforms them into output symbols – the original sentences in German – is a Turing machine. Newman turned to the Post Office at Dollis Hill in northwest London to build such a device.

By April 1943, the Post Office had built a hybrid machine – a

37

mix of vacuum tube and relay devices. It was called the 'Heath Robinson' after the cartoonist who drew famously eccentric and outlandish contraptions. (In America such machines are called Rube Goldberg devices.) These machines, however, were not sufficiently fast or reliable.

Speed was essential. The strategic value of intercepted messages faded rapidly if they were not deciphered quickly. Like Zuse and Schreyer in Germany, British engineers realized that if their decoding machines were entirely electronic they would work much faster. But what about their reliability? Most people balked at the idea of a machine made with valves, which were widely regarded as undependable.

Tommy Flowers, a Post Office engineer who before the Second World War had been involved in designing electronic telephone exchanges, disagreed. He had proven to his own satisfaction that valves offered reliability some 1000 times greater than electromechanical switches. But when Flowers suggested to Bletchley Park that they should build an entirely electronic machine with over 1000 valves his proposal was met with scepticism. Undaunted, he set out to build the machine. Working 90-hour weeks they completed the first Colossus (as it came to be called because of its size) in 11 months in December 1943. The Bletchley Park code-breakers put Colossus to the test, running a problem they had solved the previous day using a Heath Robinson.

Thomas Howard 'Tommy' Flowers

Flowers recalls that when the correct result was produced in about 30 minutes they ran the test again. Incredulous, they kept running it. 'They were taken aback, they just couldn't believe it', says Flowers. 'They had never had that order of reliability and of course, never that order of speed.'[5]

The Robinson machines had compared the message and key tapes by physically driving both tapes at high speed over a framework of pulleys to read the data. Colossus, on the other hand, stored the key in its internal vacuum tube memory, and ran only one tape – the message tape – at nearly 30 miles per hour, reading 5000 characters per second. Storing the key in its electronic memory allowed it to be altered quickly, allowing it to be free from the constraints of punching new key tapes each trial.

Colossus was the first digital computing machine to use valves on a large scale. While it had been built for a special purpose and was not easily programmable for any other task than code breaking, it showed that computers were not simply numerical machines. Colossus had computed letters rather than numbers. It showed that computers were logical machines; they transformed symbols of any kind according to a given set of rules.

Zuse had built machines that were automatic, binary, program-controlled calculators, which

39

The Colossus at Bletchley Park.

could do the work of human computers, albeit quite slowly. Colossus had proved that electronic technology could be harnessed to carry out a different computational task – cryptoanalysis – at high speed. In America, one project was finally to realize the aim of numerical calculation at electronic speed. This was the ENIAC (Electronic Numerical Integrator Analyzer and Computer). This machine would not be a full computer in the modern sense, but would demonstrate the feasibility of such machines and signal the start of the modern computer age.

The United States

The ENIAC might never have been built had it not been for the Second World War. The US military was faced with a pressing problem which, like the code breaking in England, had to be solved quickly, more quickly than humans could manage alone. A computational crisis arose at the Ballistics Research Laboratory (BRL) in Maryland in the preparation of firing tables. Artillery pieces are aimed by setting the angle of the barrel so that the shell travels the desired distance to the target. The

40

Group photograph of the ENIAC team, 1946. Eckert is on the far left; Goldstine is fourth from left; Mauchly, fifth from left.

A large mechanical analog computer, 1950s.

41

actual trajectory of the shell depends on a daunting array of physical factors – the weight of the shell, propellant charge, and air resistance. Air resistance in turn varies with temperature, humidity, altitude and the shape of the projectile. The complex trajectory equations clearly could not be solved by gunners in the field. Doing sums under fire is no fun even with a desk calculator and doctorate in applied physics.

The Ballistics Research Laboratory was responsible for producing sets of firing data – booklets of look-up tables that gave the correct settings for various conditions. A typical firing table would provide data for some 3000 trajectories each one requiring the solution of very complex mathematical equations. The computational task was monumental. The mechanical analog monsters with their rods, gears and disks, took around 30 days to complete a trajectory table. However, in comparison, a human computer with a desktop calculator took several days to compute and tabulate *a single trajectory.*

With 176 human computers and two mechanical computing analog machines, the BRL was taking about three months to churn out one firing table. For a while they kept up, but as the war intensified they fell hopelessly behind. In an attempt to catch up, the BRL established a computing substation at the Moore School of Electrical Engineering at the University of Pennsylvania in Philadelphia, to recruit and train human computers. Lieutenant Herman Goldstine was the BRL officer in charge of the Moore School venture. In a chance conversation with one of the School's computer mechanics he heard about the work of Moore School professor, John Mauchly. In 1942 Mauchly had written about the use of vacuum tubes for high speed calculation and Goldstine, constantly alert to solutions to the problem of ballistics calculations, pursued the lead.[6] The result was that on 5 June 1943, the BRL commissioned the development of what was to become the ENIAC. J Presper Eckert, a close colleague of Mauchly's, was the chief engineer, Mauchly the chief consultant and Goldstine provided supervisory liaison with BRL.

TABLE III.
DEFLECTIONS FOR 10 m.s. WIND.

L.S. = Lateral Deflection in Plane of Sight for Cross Wind.
L.A. = Lateral Deflection in Azimuth for Cross Wind.
V. = Vertical Deflection for Head or Following Wind.

Height		mils.	100	200	300	400	500	600	700	800	900	1000	1100	1200	1300	1400	1500	Height
		Deg Min.	5°-37½'	11°-15'	16°-52½'	22°-30'	28°-7½'	33°-45'	39°-22½'	45°-0'	50°-37½'	56°-15'	61°-52½'	67°-30'	73°-7½'	78°-45'	84°-22½'	
Metres										Deflection in Mils.								Metres
500	L.S.	5·2	3·2	2·6	2·3	2·2	2·1	2·0	1·9	1·9	1·9	1·9	1·9	1·9	1·9	1·8	500
	L.A.	5·2	3·2	2·7	2·5	2·5	2·5	2·6	2·7	3·0	3·4	4·0	5·0	6·5	9·7	18·4	
	V.	—	—	—	—	—	—	—	—	—	—	—	—	—	—	—	
1000	L.S.	14·4	5·7	4·1	3·4	3·0	2·7	2·5	2·4	2·3	2·3	2·3	2·2	2·2	2·1	2·1	1000
	L.A.	14·5	5·8	4·3	3·7	3·4	3·2	3·2	3·4	3·6	4·1	4·9	5·7	7·6	10·8	21·5	
	V.	0·7	0·7	0·7	0·7	0·7	0·7	0·7	0·7	0·7	0·7	0·7	0·7	0·7	0·7	0·7	
1500	L.S.	—	9·1	6·0	4·6	3·9	3·4	3·1	2·9	2·8	2·7	2·7	2·6	2·5	2·5	2·4	1500
	L.A.	—	9·3	6·3	5·0	4·4	4·1	4·0	4·1	4·4	4·9	5·7	6·8	8·6	12·8	24·5	
	V.	—	1·4	1·4	1·4	1·4	1·4	1·4	1·4	1·4	1·4	1·4	1·4	1·4	1·4	1·4	
2000	L.S.	—	14·3	8·3	6·0	4·9	4·2	3·8	3·5	3·3	3·2	3·1	3·0	2·9	2·8	2·8	3000
	L.A.	—	14·6	8·7	6·5	5·6	5·1	4·9	4·9	5·2	5·8	6·6	7·8	10·0	14·4	28·6	
	V.	—	2·1	2·1	2·1	2·1	2·1	2·1	2·1	2·1	2·1	2·1	2·1	2·1	2·1	2·1	
2500	L.S.	—	—	11·1	7·8	6·1	5·2	4·5	4·2	3·9	3·7	3·5	3·4	3·3	3·2	3·2	2500
	L.A.	—	—	11·6	8·4	6·9	6·3	5·8	5·9	6·2	6·9	7·4	8·9	11·4	16·4	32·7	
	V.	—	—	2·9	2·9	2·9	2·9	2·9	2·9	2·9	2·9	2·9	2·9	2·9	2·9	2·9	
3000	L.S.	—	—	14·6	9·9	7·6	6·3	5·4	4·9	4·5	4·2	4·0	3·9	3·8	3·7	3·6	3000
	L.A.	—	—	15·3	10·7	8·6	7·6	7·0	6·9	7·1	7·7	8·5	10·2	13·1	19·0	36·8	
	V.	—	—	3·6	3·6	3·6	3·6	3·6	3·6	3·6	3·6	3·6	3·6	3·6	3·6	3·6	
3500	L.S.	—	—	—	12·3	9·3	7·6	6·4	5·7	5·3	4·8	4·6	4·4	4·3	4·1	4·0	3500
	L.A.	—	—	—	13·3	10·5	9·1	8·3	8·1	8·4	8·6	9·8	11·5	14·8	21·0	40·9	
	V.	—	—	—	4·3	4·3	4·3	4·3	4·3	4·3	4·3	4·3	4·3	4·3	4·3	4·3	
4000	L.S.	—	—	—	15·1	11·2	8·9	7·5	6·7	6·1	5·5	5·2	4·9	4·8	4·6	4·5	4000
	L.A.	—	—	—	16·3	12·7	10·7	9·7	9·5	9·6	9·9	11·0	12·8	16·5	23·6	46·0	
	V.	—	—	—	5·0	5·0	5·0	5·0	5·0	5·0	5·0	5·0	5·0	5·0	5·0	5·0	
4500	L.S.	—	—	—	—	13·2	10·4	8·7	7·7	6·9	6·3	5·9	5·6	5·3	5·2	5·1	4500
	L.A.	—	—	—	—	15·0	12·5	11·3	10·9	10·9	11·3	12·5	14·6	18·3	26·7	52·1	
	V.	—	—	—	—	5·8	5·8	5·8	5·8	5·8	5·8	5·8	5·8	5·8	5·8	5·8	
5000	L.S.	—	—	—	—	15·7	12·2	10·1	8·8	7·9	7·1	6·6	6·2	6·0	5·8	5·7	5000
	L.A.	—	—	—	—	17·8	14·7	13·1	12·4	12·5	12·8	14·0	16·2	20·7	29·7	58·2	
	V.	—	—	—	—	6·5	6·5	6·5	6·5	6·5	6·5	6·5	6·5	6·5	6·5	6·5	

The Vertical Deflection should be applied " Up " for a Following wind, and " Down " for a Head Wind.

24   25

Above left: John Mauchly

(on the right).

Above: Vannevar Bush with

the Differential Analyzer.

Left: Herman Goldstine

(left) and Presper Eckert

holding a unit from

ENIAC.

Far left: Portion of a firing

table.

Right: Diagram of a

trajectory to a target.

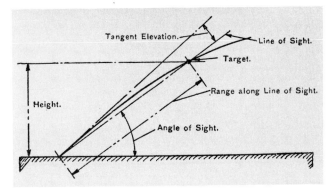

ENIAC was completed in November 1945, missing the war by several months – but it worked and it was very fast. The speed barrier which had plagued Zuse had been shattered. ENIAC could perform 5000 additions per second, 357 multiplications per second, and up to 38 divisions per second. The doom-laden predictions of unreliability because of the vast number of tubes proved, after some teething troubles, unfounded, and up to twenty hours of fault-free operation were achieved – an astonishing record by the standards of the day.

In physical terms ENIAC was a monster. It was almost 100 feet long, 8 feet high, 3 feet deep and weighed thirty tons. It contained almost 18 000 tubes, 70 000 resistors, 10 000 capacitors, 6000 switches, 1500 relays and cost a little under $500 000 – well over budget.

Apart from the staggering amount of calculation it did in its working life (including H-bomb calculations) its significance in the history of computing is that of a major milestone of achievability. Its existence was an impressive demonstration that large electronic systems were technically viable.

In contrast to Colossus which was buried in secrecy for some 30 years after the war (and to some extent still is), and to Zuse's work which was largely unknown outside Germany, ENIAC was widely publicized. In a demonstration to the press ENIAC performed 5000 additions before the reporters had time to look up at the panel lights indicating the results. Another show of ENIAC's prowess was the performance of high-speed calculations of shell trajectories. The numerical value of the height of the shell, displayed in lights, rose and fell as ENIAC whirred away. ENIAC took twenty seconds to calculate the path of a shell that would take thirty seconds to reach its target. Such prospects for high-speed prediction were not lost on the military. As for myth, ENIAC established flashing lights as the symbolic outward sign of mysterious internal activity, and every fictional computer from then on had them in abundance.

The big problem with ENIAC was that it was extremely difficult to program. ENIAC had to be set up afresh for each new problem and

Left: Technician setting switches on one of ENIAC's panels.

Right: The ENIAC, c1946.

was programmed using plug panels – matrices of sockets into which cables were plugged. Programming the machine effectively involved rewiring it. Problems which the ENIAC could solve in minutes took up to two days to program using these tedious manual connections. And the programmers included many of the same human computers, like Kay Mauchly, whom the ENIAC had made redundant. According to Kay Mauchly they had to figure out how to program ENIAC by themselves because there were no manuals, only wiring diagrams.

The stored-program

The bottleneck was now no longer computational speed but the laborious and time-consuming process of programming the machine by hand – setting switches and wiring plug-boards. The difference between the few minutes for the machine to compute a result and the days it took to set the problem up was a costly mismatch between man and machine. The last crucial link between these transitional machines and the concept of a fully-fledged modern general-purpose programmable computer was the ability to store the set of instructions – the computer's program – in internal electronic memory.

If the program *and* the data were prepared in advance and fed into the computer's memory, each new program would instantly convert the machine to the right state to carry out that program's task. A machine which calculated a missile trajectory, could, with a new program, quickly become a machine which could calculate say, the reactions of a hydrogen bomb.

With an internal stored-program, the machine could access and execute its programs at electronic speeds. But beyond considerations of speed, the stored-program idea would open up a number of possibilities, including making machines friendlier. Well before ENIAC, with its labyrinthine plug-boards, was completed, Eckert and Mauchly had conceived of this last step. Though the success of ENIAC was far from assured at that time, Goldstine again enlisted the financial support of the Ordnance Department for a new machine – a stored-program computer called EDVAC – Electronic Discrete Variable Computer. The contract for its design and construction was issued in the autumn of 1944.

EDVAC provided the logical model that has dominated the internal organization of computers since. The internal architecture of EDVAC-type machines became known as 'von Neumann' machines following events that led from a chance meeting on an Aberdeen railway platform between Goldstine and John von Neumann.

John Von Neumann was a brilliant Hungarian-American mathematician of immense intellectual stature. As a result of the Aberdeen encounter with Goldstine he visited the ENIAC project in the autumn of 1944 in time to participate in the EDVAC project. Eckert and Mauchly set about briefing the fascinated newcomer about the ENIAC. The meetings were largely about technical design rather than system architecture, internal organization or logical principles. Von Neumann went away and produced, in June 1945, an historic paper called *First Draft of a Report on the EDVAC*. The report was the first formal description of the design of a general-purpose digital

47

John von Neumann and the computer built at the Institute for Advanced Study, Princeton, New Jersey.

electronic computer and formulated the logical principles and operation of the modern stored-program computer (see box). The report was widely circulated, its impact and prestige enhanced by the standing of its author. Though EDVAC was not completed until 1952, the report was a light guiding the way for all those who after the Second World War wanted to build a fully electronic, stored-program computer.

Work on ENIAC and EDVAC established the Moore School as a Mecca of computer expertise in the immediate post-war period. Knowledge was willingly shared and one of those asked to participate in a series of lectures in the summer of 1946 was Maurice Wilkes, head of the

48

The von Neumann computer

The basic design of a computer outlined by John von Neumann in his *First Draft Report on the EDVAC* written in 1945 has dominated the design of computers ever since.

The system he described consists of four basic elements: a Memory Unit for storing data and program instructions, an Arithmetic Unit for performing numerical calculations, a Control Unit that directs the movement of information and the sequence of actions, and Input and Output units – devices for feeding information into the system and a

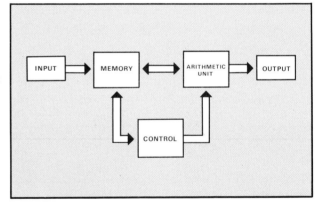

means of recording results.

Von Neumann made a strategic design decision that the computer should work serially i.e. execute instructions in a step by step fashion. Even though machines that performed more than one operation at a time were faster, von Neumann committed himself to serial operation for practical reasons – to simplify construction and reduce complexity. Until relatively recently, virtually all computers have used this basic arrangement.

University Mathematical Laboratory at Cambridge. His university brief was to develop methods of computing as well as computing machinery. On his return from the United States in the autumn he began his task inspired by his Moore School experiences. By commercial standards of research and development Wilkes had extraordinary freedom in not having to justify himself to any management authority. He recalls: 'I didn't have to ask anyone "could I build a computer please". I didn't have to put in any proposal. I didn't have to arrange any budget. I was in charge and I could go ahead. The times were extremely abnormal.'[7]

The unsolved technological problem resulting from the decision to have a stored internal program was memory. How were the programming instructions to be stored inside the machine? Valves were not the answer as the cost would be astronomical. Storing a few numbers electronically as the ENIAC had done was one thing; storing long sets of programming instructions was another. Eckert estimated that ENIAC would have needed a million valves (rather than the 18 000 they used) to store programming instructions electronically as well as for storing data.

Maurice Wilkes with mercury delay line memory.

Wilkes decided to pursue another idea suggested by Eckert: using sound waves circulating in mercury delay lines. These had been developed in radar work for storing the streams of electronic pulses that made up a

apart from Wilkes' was in the race. A group at Manchester University under Dr Freddie Williams were approaching the problem from a different angle and using the surface of a cathode ray tube, like those used in radar displays,

50

picture on a radar screen. Eckert had suggested that similar long cylinders filled with mercury could store equally well the stream of pulses that held a machine's instructions.

In Britain another team

to create a memory storage device. This idea had arisen from wartime work done at the British Radar Research Headquarters. On 21 June 1948, the Manchester team prepared and ran a test program, thereby establishing their place in history as creators of the first electronic, digital, stored-program computer. While some useful calculations were carried out on the Manchester machine, it was really a prototype. The main motivation was not to make a practical university computer so much as to discover how to build more sophisticated machines which the Manchester-based electronics company Ferranti could then mass-produce.

Although the race to build the first stored-program computer was technically won by Manchester University, it was the Cambridge University Electronic

Delay Storage Automatic Calculator (EDSAC) machine built by Wilkes (and operational by May 1949) which most historians regard as the first serious stored-program machine geared to users and capable of doing useful work. As used by the Manchester computer, the stored-program made many aspects of the process faster and simpler. But at Cambridge they exploited the key advantage the stored-program offered – making the computer easier to use.

Left: The Manchester Mark I.

Below: An EDSAC with queue of users.

51

52

The digital electronic computer was a practical embodiment of a Universal Turing Machine; it could simulate any computing machine. It followed therefore that it could simulate a friendlier computer. The beginnings of this had been grasped by von Neumann in his *First Draft*. When addressing the problems of converting decimal numbers into binary – a tedious, repetitive error-prone process – von Neumann had seen that, since this was just a computation, the computer could do it. The computer was thus preprocessing one part of its input – the data. But, it followed that if one part of the input could be computed, why not the other part – the programming instructions themselves? At Manchester programs had to be written in binary code – a laborious, unintuitive and error-prone process. A process crying out to be computed by the computer itself.

Wilkes realized that the stored-program offered more than just speed and convenience – it offered the chance to make the computer easier to use, a development that he believed would attract users. The Cambridge machine could be programmed using an alphabetic shorthand, which programmers found much easier to write than the 0s and 1s of binary code. The computer automatically translated these instructions into a binary code that it (the computer) could understand. They rapidly developed a library of tapes for frequently used routines which scientists could use. Wilkes had invented the user.

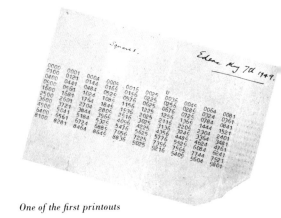

One of the first printouts from EDSAC, 7 May 1949.

It is of some philosophical interest that with the stored-program, the distinction between data and program becomes blurred. The *data* for the program which actually converts the programmer's shorthand code in to 0s and 1s is itself a computer program. The output expressed in binary code is another program – one which the

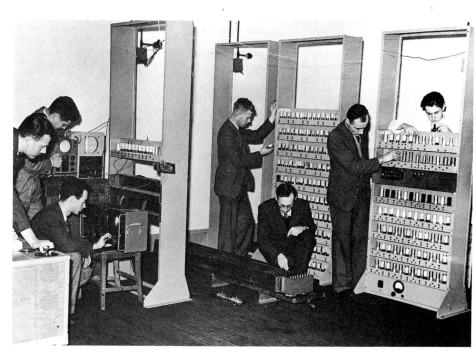

EDSAC during construction, 1947.

machine can execute. Once inside the computer's memory, program and data can (to some extent) be treated interchangeably. A program can become data and data can become a program. This allows enormous versatility and flexibility which ENIAC could never have achieved.

The stored-program concept was a critical breakthrough because it offered the chance to make computers easier to use. As we shall see, the advent of higher level programming languages and friendly user interfaces depended on this crucial step.

Wilkes called his machine EDSAC and the similarity of the acronym to the Moore School EDVAC acknowledged the transatlantic influence. EDSAC I offered a regular computing service to the university from early 1950 until it was shut down in 1958, and was used by many scientific disciplines. For some emerging sciences the computer was soon seen not as a luxury but as an essential. In radioastronomy an enhanced EDSAC, EDSAC II, was an integral part of the first radio telescope, which was made from combining a pair of German radar dishes. At the same time, in molecular biology, EDSACs were used to work out the three-dimensional structure of myoglobin – one of the first of two giant proteins to be described in atomic detail.

The first scientists to use EDSAC and other computers in the early 1950s continued to view them as numerical machines. There was one notable exception – Alan Turing. After the Second World War, Turing wrote a report outlining a proposal for a new British digital computer, which would be called the Automatic Computing Engine (ACE).[8] It is clear that his understanding of the computer went far beyond that of his contemporaries, partly because he had invented the computer in thought a decade before. For Turing the electronic pulses were arbitrary electronic tokens which the machine shuffled according to physical law without any understanding of what they represented. The notion of the stored-program was natural to him not just because it would yield greater speed. The machine did not know the difference between a number and a program instruction; all it cared about were pulses. It would be possible then to represent instructions in binary code and store them in the machine together with numbers because to the machine they were indistinguishable. These instructions could embody the rules of chess, the rules for retrieving filing cards and even the rules plotting a missile trajectory – in short, they covered anything you could effectively describe as a procedure.

As Turing said in a lecture shortly afterwards: 'Some years ago I… considered a type of machine which had a central mechanism, and an infinite memory which was contained on an infinite tape… Machines such as the ACE may be regarded as practical versions of this same type of machine… We may say that the universal machine is one which, when supplied with the appropriate instructions, can be made to do any rule of thumb process. This feature is paralleled in digital computing machines such as the ACE. They are in fact practical versions of the universal machine… When any particular problem has to be handled, the appropriate instructions for the computing process involved are stored in the memory of the ACE and it is then "set up" for carrying out that process.'[9]

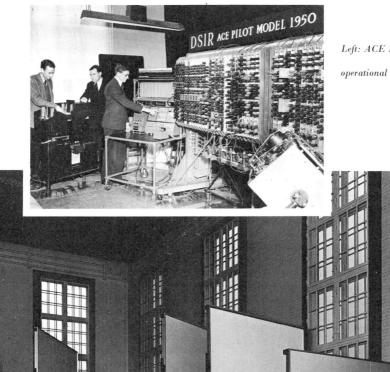

Left: ACE Pilot computer,

operational in 1950.

Above: ACE computer,

operational in 1957.

Standing for Automatic Computing Engine, ACE was a graceful acknowledgement to Babbage, whose place in history had yet to be fully recognized. The full-size computer Turing helped design was to have been the test bed for his ideas about the way such computing machines might mirror the workings of the human mind. Turing, like Babbage, never saw his machine completed, and even the smaller version of the ACE was not finished until after he had left the project to write programs for the Manchester machine.

Turing loved to speculate about thinking machines and the limits of what they could do. Many engineers, who were simply trying to build a functioning machine, found such talk flippant, and even outlandish. But Turing did win the attention of a wider audience, giving popular talks including one on BBC radio. In 1950 he wrote a seminal paper in the philosophy journal *Mind* entitled 'Computing Machinery and Intelligence' which, as we shall see in a later chapter, still looms over the community of researchers pursuing the quest of artificial intelligence.

Turing died in 1954, at the age of 41, his death officially ruled as suicide. His fascinating life has been the subject of several books and a highly successful play. Had he lived, however, he would doubtless have been amazed at the impact of his universal machines. The digital computer would eventually shed its numerical stigma and find truly general use and application, but it would take another 30 years.

Before the Second World War when people had used the word computer they were talking about a person. After 1946, the term usually referred to a machine with certain features which set it apart from other machines. It was automatic, general-purpose, electronic, digital and binary, and had a stored internal program. If this new invention was merely an exceptionally fast arithmetic machine, it followed that the world would only ever need a few of them. After all, one machine could do the work of 10 000 human computers with calculators. In the post-war electronic era there were suggestions that Britain would need just three or four computers and the United States six at most. With such a tiny potential market, almost everybody doubted that there was any money to be made out of building them. They would be proved wrong. The computer was poised to infiltrate industry. The first stage in its relentless advance would be to take over the calculator and data processing industries which had burgeoned in the pre-electronic years.

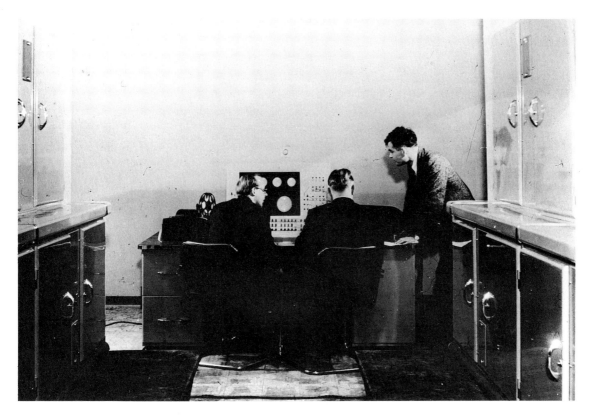

Manchester Mark I computer. Alan Turing is on the right leaning on the console.

$\mathcal{A}$n industry is born

Before the advent of electronic computers the office machine industry had a flourishing calculator industry and a data processing industry which supplied a variety of tabulating machines for managing information. Armies of clerks toiled at these tabulating machines feeding in sets of punch cards, sorting them, taking the cards to other machines and printing out tables of data. The ritualized procedure was as 'mechanical' as had been the actions of human computers doing calculations before and during the war. In the years ahead it would be realized that if a computer could follow the instructions to take, store and manipulate numbers, then it could also follow instructions to take, store and manipulate non-numerical information like names and addresses. Computers would change forever the way the world did business and, in doing so, would themselves become one of the largest and most powerful industries in the world.

The business history of the electronic computer began in 1946, when J Presper Eckert and John Mauchly, the inventors of the ENIAC, tried to patent their invention. The Moore School had recently introduced a policy that patent rights for all inventions made at the School should belong to the University of Pennsylvania. But Mauchly and Eckert refused to sign a release giving the University exclusive rights to the technology of the ENIAC, and they left the school in March 1946, less than a month after the ENIAC's public unveiling.

Their departure marked the end of the University of Pennsylvania's lead in computer development. Had the 28-year-old engineer and 40-year-old mathematician stayed in academia, computer history might be told differently. But the two chose an unconventional route. Why not, they thought, start a computer company?

In 1946, success in the computer business seemed about as likely as putting a man on the moon. The ENIAC was the only large-scale electronic calculating machine in the world. A handful of institutions, mostly universities, had plans to build stored-program computers, but these were to be for scientific use. Eckert and Mauchly's decision seemed foolhardy at best. And as Eckert recalls, finding investors in the project proved all but impossible: 'We went over to New York and talked to people in Wall Street and they just couldn't see it at that time. So we decided to try to do it on our own and my father signed a note at the bank for $25 000, which helped us get started.'

Swimming against the tide, Eckert and Mauchly started the first electronic computer business in the world – the Electronic Control Company, in Philadelphia, Pennsylvania, and set about finding buyers for

59

their product. One organization was desperate enough to take a chance – the US Census Bureau.

In 1945, a worried Census Bureau was looking ahead to the 1950 census. It had great numbers of clerks with tabulating machines but was still drowning in paper – its records filled a football field. The Hollerith technology which had saved it 50 years before had reached its limit. To fulfil its Congressional mandate to finish the census within 10 years it needed a new machine. When Mauchly and Eckert turned up claiming they could solve all the bureau's problems with an electronic computer they found a receptive audience. Morris Hanson, the Assistant Director for Statistical Standards, recalls that he and his colleagues thought 'it was 'magic. We couldn't believe it was really feasible to begin with [but] as we talked more and more with them we came to believe that they knew what they were talking about.'

After a few months, the first contract for a commercial computer was signed with the US Census Bureau on 25 September 1946. The two scientists who had spent all their lives in academia were uncertain how to budget the project, so agreed to make it for a price they knew the Census Bureau could afford – exactly $350 270.

The machine was to be called the Universal Automatic Computer (UNIVAC) and work on it began in October 1946. But in less than a year, Eckert and Mauchly were badly behind schedule and seriously in debt. It was a pattern they would repeat time and time again. For the next two and a half years they would struggle to keep their company afloat.

But Eckert and Mauchly were not the only ones who believed the computer had a future in business. Three thousand miles away in London, a seemingly unlikely company prepared to take its first steps into the computer age – J Lyons & Company Ltd., a wholesale food and catering business that ran some 150 tea shops, and several hotels and restaurants.

Lyons were always looking to improve operations and had even recruited two top Cambridge mathematics graduates – Raymond Thompson and John Simmons – in their drive to make clerical operations more efficient. It is not surprising then that newspaper accounts of the 'Giant Brain' (the ENIAC) at the University of Pennsylvania intrigued Lyons' top management and led them to wonder if this was the machine they had been waiting for.

After seeking advice from experts, Lyons decided it was an EDVAC-type computer they wanted. But they could find no company in Britain to build one. With Maurice Wilkes' help, Thompson and Simmons took on the job themselves and began work on LEO, the Lyons Electronic Office, in 1949.

Lyons predicted that the computer would cost £25 000 and would save the company half that amount each year, handling the ordering and supply of some 40 000 different

A. J. Lyons & Co. Ltd tea shop

products to the 150 tea shops. These estimates proved overly optimistic.

The first steps towards a computer industry had been taken on both sides of the Atlantic. But with what chance of success? Despite the enthusiasm of Eckert and Mauchly in America and the LEO team in Britain, good reasons existed for doubting that computers had a commercial future.

LEO I monitor desk

First, there was the question of reliability. In the early days, the valve was widely believed to be one of the most fragile of all electronic components. It was considered too undependable and to have too short a working life to be soldered into circuits like other components, so it was slotted in like a light bulb. It was assumed that from time to time valves would burn out and need replacing and indeed the ENIAC with 18 000 valves had needed teams of people to carry out this task. How could a commercial product be based on such a vulnerable component? In practice this weakness was not as serious as first feared. Most 'burn outs' happened when the valves were turned on or off. Eckert discovered that leaving the machine on constantly even when it was not being used, greatly reduced the number of blow outs.

But there were other, more compelling arguments against commercial computing. One concerned the purpose of computers. The attention of many of the key scientists who were developing computers (and that of their military paymasters), was focused solely on the ability of the new machine to do complex scientific calculations quickly. Computers had done computations of superhuman proportions such as mathematically modelling the H-bomb. This program was run in November 1945. But, it was argued, the number of such giant problems was small and it seemed reasonable that only a handful of computers would be needed.

Another more telling objection concerned the running of the computer. Even assuming that one could raise the money to build a computer, humans were needed to program it. In those days this meant being able to talk to the machine in its own arcane binary language of 0s and 1s. A computer centre might require 20 or so mathematicians to service it, mediating between scientist and machine.[1] The shortage of such key personnel was seen as a fundamental brake on progress. Also, whereas the computer operated at superhuman speeds, human beings spent days casting the problem. Computers hardly seemed practical.

Bringing the computer to market

Convincing as these arguments were, they did not stop Lyons or Eckert and Mauchly. As Eckert strove to develop reliable computer hardware, Mauchly searched desperately for customers prepared to invest in the future. By 1948, they had four – the US Census Bureau, Northrop Aircraft Corporation, Prudential Life Insurance and the AC Neilsen Company (best known today for their work in television ratings.[2]) Mauchly had convinced each that it had much to gain from a computer. Whatever the task – aircraft calculations, actuarial tables, policy valuations or market research statistics – Mauchly argued, the computer could do the job more quickly and efficiently than clerks grinding away at tabulating machines. But convincing customers to pay the true price was difficult and in each case, they wound up building the machine for a fixed price. Because Eckert and Mauchly were pioneering many new technologies, like magnetic tape for

63

data storage, and had to overcome unforeseen problems, the fixed prices of these contracts soon began to look unrealistically low. After two years in business, the newly renamed Eckert-Mauchly Computer Company was almost bankrupt.

In late 1948, help came from a most unlikely source – The American Totalizator Company (AMTOTE), makers of the mechanical equipment that calculates odds and displays pay-offs at race tracks. Harry Straus, the founder and general manager of AMTOTE, fearing that the new electronic computer might render their machines obsolete, purchased a 40 per cent interest in the Eckert-Mauchly Computer Corporation.

But this proved only a reprieve. In October 1949, Harry Straus was killed in a plane crash. The owners of the company, the Munn brothers, had never believed in computers and the following month pulled out of the deal. Eckert and Mauchly looked for other investors but eventually realized that their only option was to sell out to the first reasonable offer.

64

Top: Harry Straus
Bottom left & right:
American Totalizator
Company.

1 *Previous page: Charles Babbage's Difference Engine No. 2. Designed in the late 1840s and built to original designs by the Science Museum, London in 1991.*

2 *Left: Charles Babbage (1860) aged 68.*

3 *Below left: A test model of the Analytical Engine*

under construction at the time of Babbage's death in 1871.

4 *Below: Punched cards for Charles Babbage's Analytical Engine.*

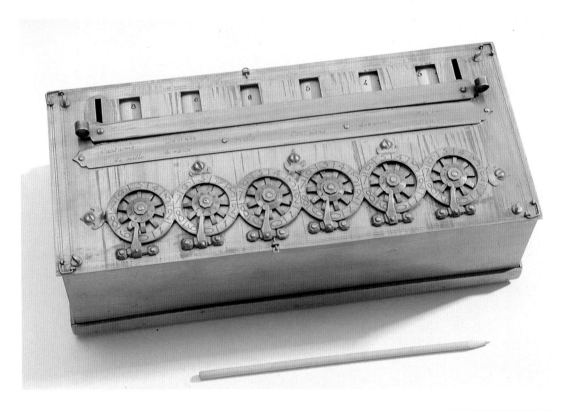

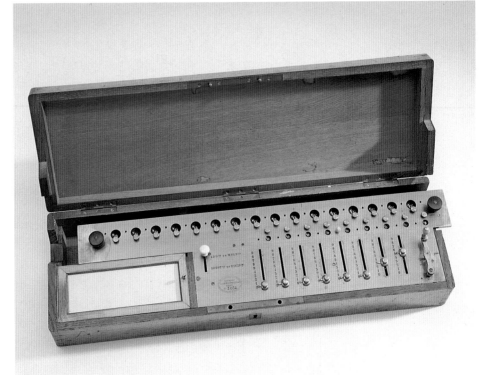

5 Top: Blaise Pascal's
calculator (replica).

6 Right: De Colmar
Arithmometer, introduced
in the 1820s.

7 Far right: Ada, Countess
of Lovelace, 1835,
aged 19.

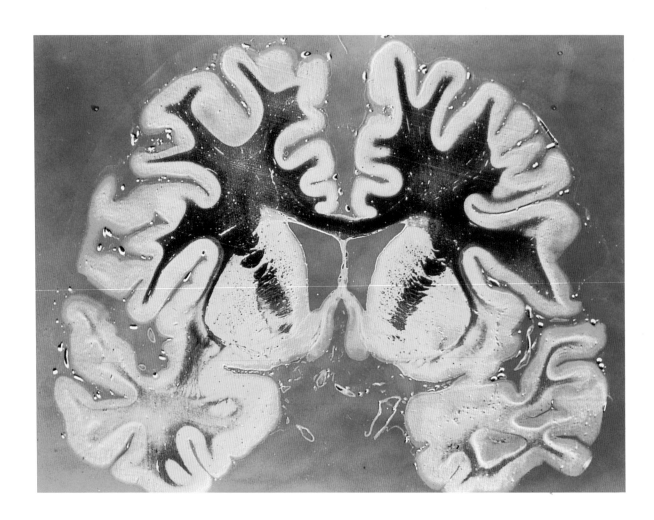

8 Above: Section through
   human brain (not true
   colour).

9 Right: Silicon chip at the
   centre of a web of metal
   connections.

10 Following page: Some of
    the wiring in the
    Connection Machine.

That offer came from Remington Rand. In 1950, Remington Rand was one of the largest business machine companies in the United States. Their products included typewriters, filing cabinets, electric razors and punched card tabulating machines. Buying a computer company, they thought, would strengthen their position in the new field of electronics. On 1 February 1950, the Eckert-Mauchly Computer Company was made a subsidiary of Remington Rand. This marked the first time a large, established company entered the computer business in the United States. Eckert and Mauchly received a total of $200 000 for their company and a guarantee of eight years' employment at Remington Rand.

One year later, the world's first two working business

computers were unveiled. In Britain on 15 February, the LEO computer was shown to Princess Elizabeth although it would not be fully operational until the autumn of that year. And it would be at least two years before LEOs came off the production line. Lyons used the LEO to compute the optimum mix for their various brands of tea, to process the payroll

Above: LEO II, introduced in 1957.

Below: LEO III, introduced in 1962.

and do tax tables. It could calculate an employee's wages and deductions in about one and a half seconds, whereas a clerk took about eight minutes. Also in 1951, in America, the first UNIVAC (which had been commissioned back in 1946) was delivered to the US Census Bureau – 15 months late and substantially over budget.

Although the contract price was $350 270, the ultimate cost of constructing the first US commercial computer has been estimated at almost $1 million. Would this be a loss leader for a huge commercial market? Remington Rand knew they had to tell people about computers and what they could do.

Above: UNIVAC on election night, 1952. Voting results are typed in and stored on the tape units.

Charles Collingwood, newscaster in the CBS studios on election night, 1952.

In an inspired marketing move, Remington Rand's UNIVACs were introduced to the American people on national television. On 4 November 1952, millions of Americans tuned into CBS to watch the presidential election results. What they found was a new analyst called UNIVAC. The reporters were Walter Cronkite, Charles Collingwood and Art Draper.

66 *Cronkite*: And now let's turn to that miracle of the modern age, the electronic brain UNIVAC and Charles Collingwood.

Collingwood: This is the face of a UNIVAC. UNIVAC is a fabulous electronic machine which we have borrowed to help us predict this election from the basis of early returns as they come in. UNIVAC is going to try to predict the winner for us just as early as we can possibly get the returns in. 99

As commentator Charles Collingwood described how the UNIVAC worked, Remington Rand employees were gathering statistics and inputting data from the early results. At 9:00 p.m. Collingwood was scheduled to announce UNIVAC's prediction of which candidate would win: Adlai Stevenson or General Dwight Eisenhower.

66 *Collingwood*: Can you say something UNIVAC? Have you got anything to say to the television audience? You're a very impolite

machine, I must say, but he's an awfully rapid calculator. There he goes.

But then UNIVAC suddenly stopped.

Collingwood: What's he saying? I think he's saying hi!... UNIVAC, can you tell me what your prediction is on the basis of the returns that we've had so far? Have you got a prediction UNIVAC?

Nothing happened.

Collingwood: I don't know. I think that UNIVAC is probably an honest machine – a good deal more honest than a lot of commentators who are working and he doesn't think he's got enough to tell us anything yet.

But UNIVAC did have enough data to make a prediction. Just before CBS went on the air UNIVAC had predicted that Eisenhower would win by a landslide. The problem was that no

Walter Cronkite, CBS anchorman, being briefed by operator at the console in preparation for election night, 1952.

68

one believed it because all the polls had said this was a tight race. Eckert was told to reprogram the computer, to come up with a 'more reasonable' estimate. A chastened UNIVAC still predicted an Eisenhower victory, but this time by a much closer margin.

When it emerged that UNIVAC had been right all along CBS had to come clean.

> *Collingwood*: Art, what happened there when we came out with that funny prediction?
> *Draper:* Well we had a lot of troubles tonight. Strangely enough, they were all human and not the machine. As more votes came in, the odds came back and it was obviously evident that we should have had nerve enough to believe the machine in the first place. It was right. We were wrong. Next year, we'll believe it.

Headlines the next day ranged from 'Machine Makes Monkey Out of Man' to 'Big Electronic Gadget Proves Machines Smarter Than Men'. UNIVAC became an overnight sensation. The word UNIVAC became synonymous with computers as 'Fri-

gidaire' had earlier become the term used for all refrigerators. UNIVACs quickly found their way into popular culture as well, and were even featured in cartoons.

Enter Big Blue

When Remington Rand had delivered the first UNIVAC to the Census Bureau, and then gone on to publicize the machine widely, there was one company that took special notice. This was Remington Rand's closest competitor, a company which had shown little or no interest in business computers until this point: International Business Machines or IBM. For nearly 50 years IBM had supplied tabulating machines to the US Census Bureau. Losing such a customer caught the company completely off-guard. And when Remington Rand began getting other orders, Thomas Watson Jr, newly appointed vice-president of IBM and son of the company's president, recalls that he 'felt a sense of great panic and... [we] had a late night conference saying this is the beginning of the end for the

69

IBM company unless we recognize [the computer] and do something about it.'[3]

Tom Watson Jr had seen that practically everything IBM made from tabulators to calculating machines could be replaced by computers. This new electronic technology was now the hottest thing in office automation and if IBM did not get involved other companies like Remington Rand would take advantage. It was not a question of keeping up with the competition but of being wiped out altogether.

Nothing was done at IBM without the approval of Thomas Watson Sr, who had served as the company's uncontested leader since 1914.

70

Left: The Bundy Time Recorder, one of the companies in the CTR conglomerate. CTR (Computing-Tabulating-

Recording Corporation) changed its name to IBM 1924.

Top right: First Tabulating Machine factory, Washington DC, 1889.

71

Far left: Thomas J Watson (right) with George Fairchild, chairman of CTR.

Top: Administration building at IBM factory, Endicott, New York. Decorated for a sales convention.

Bottom: Quitting time at International Time Recording Company, Endicott, 1918. ITR, which manufactured employee time clocks, was part of the CTR conglomerate.

He was against IBM making business computers. IBM had a vast number of customers (including the Census Bureau until recently) who bought punch card machines and tabulators. Why invest in technology which might persuade customers to stop buying those machines? A dominating personality, Watson Sr had created a culture of 'yes' men around him who were too frightened for their jobs to take a stand. Forward-looking executives who knew that the computer had to be embraced gathered around Tom Watson Jr, the one person who could not be easily cowed or fired by the old man.

The key to persuading old Mr Watson to allow IBM to make computers lay in his patriotism. In times of war he traditionally put his company at the service of the US government. The Korean War was no different and he put his son in charge of IBM's defence activities. Watson Jr dispatched two emissaries to government installations to ask them what they most needed from IBM. They

Far left: Thomas J Watson, Sr

Left: Watson Sr, delivering

a morale-boosting speech at

a sales convention in 1918.

Below: Watson Sr,

addressing a sales class,

1929.

73

came back with one answer — computers. Unable to refuse, Watson Sr allowed construction of a scientific computer called the Defense Calculator, or 701, which was unveiled in April 1953. IBM had entered the computer business.

At the time, IBM's success in the computer business was by no means assured. They had a lot of catching up to do. In Britain, LEO was in general service (Lyons would soon set up a special company to market them to other businesses). In America, as IBM installed its first four computers, Remington Rand (which merged with the Sperry Company in 1955), had seven machines installed and orders for 16 more. If there was a leading computer company, it was Remington Rand.

But IBM did some shrewd marketing. After bringing out a commercial version of the defence calculator, the company went on to develop, in 1954, an inexpensive business computer called the 650. It was the first moderately priced mass-produced computer and, more importantly, the machine fitted seamlessly into existing punch card installations,

which customers were familiar with. (By contrast, Remington Rand used magnetic tape to store data. While this was the way forward, it involved the customer in a bigger change.) The 650 sent a confident message to customers that IBM would guide them gently into the future. The IBM 650 turned out to be the Model T of computers and within a couple of years, orders for them had climbed to more than 1000. Other models followed, like the 1401, which were even more successful.

By 1956, when Thomas Watson Sr died, IBM was no longer just a tabulator company, but the world's largest and most profitable computer manufacturer. In the years ahead IBM would dominate the market. This had much to do with their brilliant, if somewhat aggressive, sales policy.

The machine, which after the Second World War had been seen as an exotic, fabulously expensive scientific research tool, had undergone a metamorphosis. It was no longer all that exotic, it was not so terribly expensive and it apparently had many uses not only in science and engineering but also in business. Advertisements of the period pushed the computer as the machine which could help expanding businesses become vastly more efficient. As innovations like magnetic tape storage became standard, the computer became increasingly seen as the crucial ingredient of a prosperous future.

There was only one problem. In practice computers could not do most of the things people were claiming, because there were not enough people to program them.

The first software crisis

Computers might now be reliable, but to be useful they had to be programmed to carry out particular tasks, like payrolls or inventory management. Sceptics had pointed out that 'programmers', as they came to be known, were in short supply. Writing programs was laborious and error-prone. In the mid to late 1950s it began to emerge that devising these complex programs cost two, three or even four times the price of the machine itself. Worse, computers costing thousands of dollars a month would sit idle, while programmers struggled to write arcane incantations for them to follow. Programs came to be called software to contrast them from the hardware of the computer itself.

Computers cannot carry out programs written in everyday English. They require a special code called machine code. Machine code is almost invariably binary code – one that recognizes only two distinct states – 'on' or 'off', true or false, '1' or '0', hi or lo. With this simple code it is possible to express decimal numbers like 1,2,3, letters of the alphabet, logical and arithmetic commands. (The number 23 in binary is 10111 for example.) The 0s and 1s of binary code make it suited to computers with thousands of small electronic switches. But what works well for computers does not work well for people.

For people who are used to the decimal system, writing in binary does not come easily. For long programs with thousands of instructions the task is near-impossible. To get around this, in the early 1950s

75

programmers developed shorthand notations called assembly code which made their work easier. With assembly code programmers could use commands like ADD to signify a regularly used operation like adding. The computer took lists of such statements under the control of another program, and faultlessly translated them into binary and executed them.

For the programmer, assembly code was an improvement but still not easy. As a useful program involved thousands of lines of code, the risk of making an error was still very high. Programmers worked long and tedious hours trying to create programs knowing that their first attempts would almost certainly fail. They spent hours trying to find their errors – a process called debugging. The job attracted few people, and a serious shortage of programmers added to a mounting software crisis. Jean Sammet, an American software pioneer, puts it like this: 'The shortage of programmers could, in the worst case, have caused the growth of the computer industry to come to a dead halt. Without programmers you don't have programs, that is to say,

software. And without software the computer is useless; you might just as well have an automobile without a driver. It just doesn't go anywhere. It just sits there.'

It became clear that the software crisis could be solved only by making programming easier – to create so-called higher level languages closer to human language. The first such language to be widely used was called FORTRAN. Although it was some way from everyday English, it allowed scientists to write statements and equations in a way to which they were accustomed. Much less technical was COBOL, designed for business applications. Human experts solve problems by using a set of abstractions, of which algebra is one. By creating computer languages which used such abstractions, programmers could tackle harder problems more quickly.

As with assembly code, the computer had to have some way to translate these high-level FORTRAN or COBOL commands into binary code. A piece of software called a compiler was the key. It took the FORTRAN or COBOL source program and 'compiled' it into code which the computer could execute. Writing a compiler was difficult, but it only had to be done once. Once a COBOL compiler had been written for a particular machine, anybody capable of writing COBOL could then write software for that computer. From this point on, programmers did not even need to know how the machines worked, nor did they need to be mathematicians. They simply had to understand what they wanted to program and how to express it in COBOL, FORTRAN or one of the many other semi-friendly languages which emerged.

By 1960, every one of the reasons for doubting the advance of computing had been overturned. Computers had proved reliable, many uses had been found for them, and simpler ways had been found to program them. Companies which previously had been content to use tabulating machines for payrolls, discovered they could use computers for sophisticated tasks from statistical analysis to market research.

The uncomplaining employee

In the 1950s the Bank of America, headquartered in San Francisco, California, was the largest bank in the world. By the middle of the decade they were processing 12 million checks daily. Sorting and recording the checks, which was mostly done by female high school graduates, was extremely tedious. Checks had no numbers, only signatures, and were filed alphabetically. The work was so unpleasant that on average, a girl stayed only nine months. Because the work was boring, mistakes were common. The bank wanted to expand personal checking accounts and realized they needed to automate. Otherwise, they estimated that within five years they would have to hire one-third of all high school graduates in California just to sort checks. For the Bank of America, like the Census Bureau before it, the computer was the answer to their prayers.

The bank hired the Stanford Research Institute, a research organization, which devised the

77

78

Electronic Recording Method of Accounting (ERMA). With ERMA, account numbers discretely placed on each check were printed in magnetic ink which could be read and sorted by machine.[4] The first ERMA system was completed in 1959 by General Electric. Using a popular actor called Ronald Reagan, GE announced ERMA's debut: 'This is Los Angeles and I'm Ronald Reagan... A competent experienced bookkeeper using conventional mechanical equipment is expected to do the sorting and posting for about 250 accounts an hour. ERMA can sort and post 500 accounts a minute.'

Automated check sorting was a tremendous success. By 1967, eight years after ERMA's launch, 95 per cent of all banks in the United States used computers to handle their checking accounts. In 1961, the Bank of America stopped hiring book-keepers; ERMA had replaced 2332 of them. Such statistics alarmed people, provoking a national debate about the impact of computers on society.

A rash of documentaries in the United States and Britain high-lighted the controversy. A celebrated programme called *The Awesome Servant* began with a picture of a robot and the commentary: 'Situation wanted: Highly efficient semi-skilled worker. Strength unlimited. Memory, photographic. Ability to adjust, excellent. Workday, 24 hours, seven days a week. No pay raises, no vacations, no coffee breaks.' The commentator continued: 'Compare the qualifications of this worker, an industrial robot, with your own. And ask yourself how that might appeal to your boss.'

For the public, these machines conjured up conflicting emotions. For some people, they meant progress, the future, and relief from tedious tasks. For others, computers inspired awe, disdain, even fear. In the film *Desk Set*, Katharine Hepburn plays the head of a newspaper reference library whose existence seems threatened by the introduction of a computer called EMERAC. Spencer Tracy plays the scientist who programs EMERAC to perform tasks faster than the staff.

The criticism caught IBM by surprise. Tom Watson Jr, who had committed IBM's future to the computer – the paragon of automation –

Spencer Tracy and
Katharine Hepburn in
Desk Set.

tried to calm the public's fears: 'A lot of these people call these machines giant brains and when I hear the term I shudder, because they are giant tools ... not giant brains, and if you have giant tools you're upgrading men not downgrading them.'

As he spoke, IBM were embarking on a mammoth project to make computers even more prevalent. They had decided to risk their considerable lead in electronic computers on the largest private venture in America's history. The scheme added 60 000 employees to IBM's payroll, required five new plants in the United States and abroad and cost $5 billion – more than twice what it cost the government to develop the atomic bomb.

A family of six computers – the System/360 – was built so that each could use the same software and peripheral equipment such as printers and tape drives. They could serve both scientific and business purposes. The hope was that the System/360 computers would be the only computers anyone would need.

Watson announced their launch on 7 April 1964, and within a year it was clear that the gamble had paid off. By the end of the 1970s, IBM 360s would be found everywhere: in universities and hospitals, in libraries and in banks. They became *the* insti-

80

tutional mainframe computer and put IBM so far ahead of other computer companies that several, in particular GE and RCA, pulled out of the business. The 360s marked the arrival of a mature computer industry. By its very size IBM had forced standardization on the industry. IBM's name was now synonymous with the computer, the icon of Orwellian power.

Like all giant corporations, it would be accused of hin-

IBM System 360 model 65

computer system.

dering progress and stifling competition. According to Ted Nelson, the colourful American author of a book called *Computer Lib*, the IBM 360: set 'civilization back about 10 years.'

"It was a brilliant marketing move to head off the other computer companies from establishing a niche within corporate America by bamboozling corporations into thinking that one computer could be used for all types of jobs. Now of course the joke is that the one IBM 360 cost as much as four or five or six [other] computers would have cost but that's not what showed up on the alleged bottom line. And so this brought about the incredibly horrific system of oppression which kept computing in its iron grip for the next decade, specifically the computer centers which were the captive tools of IBM, where not only did you have to use the computer according to the system that had been laid out and submit punch cards, but also you had to do it according to the rules laid down by the bureaucracy that ran it who were all trained by and extremely loyal to IBM even though they worked for your corporation allegedly."

Oppressive or not, IBM's strategy worked. By the mid-1980s, the System 360 and its direct descendants had accounted for more than a hundred billion dollars in revenue for IBM, earning more in profits than all of its competitors combined.

The British computer industry, started by Lyons in the late 1940s, never had a chance. In 1963, after selling only 100 computers, Lyons sold their computer division to the English Electric Company. By then they found it almost impossible to compete with American companies like IBM. After several mergers, the English Electric Company would be absorbed into ICL, the descendent of the British Tabulating Machine Company founded in 1907. In 1990, Fujitsu bought 80 per cent of ICL.

But IBM's hegemony was not to go unchallenged. In the next 20 years the popular image of the computer would change drastically. The hardware would evolve from a mysterious machine that filled a room, to a small personal computer that could fit on a desk or in someone's lap. Huge improvements in software would change perceptions of what a computer was for. The computer would be viewed less and less as an Orwellian symbol of control and more as a versatile tool of individual empowerment.

IBM's Defense Calculator, renamed the IBM 701, unveiled in April 1953.

83

S ilicon dreams

The makers of the ENIAC had been compelled to use digital electronics for reasons of speed and accuracy. In 1946 the thermionic valve or vacuum tube was the only switching technology that could work fast enough to do the calculations of missile trajectories within a reasonable time. But these valves, which were used in everything from radios to Geiger counters, were large, expensive and consumed a great deal of power. When thousands of valves were connected inside a machine, enormous heat was given off.

A year after the ENIAC was unveiled to the public, an historic discovery was made at Bell Telephone Laboratories. On 23 December 1947, three Bell scientists, William Shockley, Walter Brattain and John Bardeen, demonstrated an invention – the transistor – which would spell the end of the valve. Unlike the fragile, power-hungry valve, the transistor was made from tiny pieces of material called semiconductors, of which germanium and silicon are the best known. By moving electronic charges

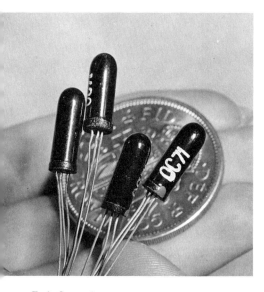

Early Germanium transistors, late 1950s.

along special paths inside a solid block of semiconductor, transistors could amplify signals and act as switches just like a valve. Minute and speedy, the transistor consumed comparatively little electricity.

Transistors became the symbol of the new electronic era and were used in a wide array of consumer products including televisions and transistor radios. From the late 1950s they also began to appear in computers. But as transistors spread into more goods, engineers spotted a fundamental difficulty which threatened to limit the progress of all complex electronics. Just as aviators had come up against the sound barrier, so the trailblazers of electronics faced an obstacle known as the tyranny of numbers.

85

The tyranny of numbers

The tyranny of numbers was the name given to the problems engineers encountered making ever more sophisticated electronic circuits. The more transistors, resistors and capacitors they put in a circuit, the more connections they had to wire. A circuit twice as large might involve four times as many connections. With traditional circuits consisting of thousands of discrete components, each part had to be individually soldered onto a circuit board, and the circuit boards had to be wired to each other. The time and labour involved in wiring accounted for most of the cost of making a circuit.

The tyranny of numbers posed another problem. Each additional connection made the entire circuit less reliable. This was of critical concern to the military. Some of the electronic devices used for guidance in military planes had as many as 20 000 transistors. The connections between the transistors, sturdy enough for work on the ground, often broke in flight. On average, every 70 hours one of the connections would come loose, sometimes with disastrous results. Engineers in the military, and at most of the semiconductor companies, were frantically searching for a remedy. In essence, unless a way could be found to eliminate the tedious process of wiring together circuits, the progress of the ultimate electronic device – the digital computer – was in jeopardy.

The physical size of machines presented a further barrier. More powerful computers required additional components. Apart from the explosion in the number of connections, the distance that signals had to travel within the machine limited the computer's speed. In a billionth of a second, a signal travelling at the speed of light (186 000 miles per second) covers nearly a foot. Some large computers built at the height of the vacuum tube era, the ATLAS in the early 1960s for example, had *miles* of wiring. Loss of speed was the price paid for greater size, because after a point, bigger machines meant diminishing returns.

The search for a solution was given top priority in industry. The first was proposed in 1952, by G W Dummer, a radar expert from Britain's Royal Radar Establishment. Presenting a paper in Washington DC, he said:

“ With the advent of the transistor, and the work of semiconductors generally, it seems now possible to envisage electronic equipment in *a solid block* with no connecting wires. The block may consist of layers of insulating, conducting, rectifying and amplifying materials, the electrical functions being connected directly by cutting out areas of the various layers.[1]

Dummer had hit on the solution that years later became known as the monolithic idea, but the prototype he built did not work and in Britain he received little support for his research.

Six years after Dummer's speech, two engineers in the United States would succeed where Dummer had failed thereby setting off a string of events that would eventually catapult the computer into a new era and establish a region of northern California as the electronics capital of the world.

The silicon gold rush

The start of the silicon rush was signalled by the arrival in 1955 of William Shockley, a co-inventor of the transistor. Shockley had returned to his native California to set up a company to produce transistors and make his fortune. Shockley began scouting for the most ambitious and

bright young engineers he could find – risk takers, technological daredevils with unshakable confidence. One he invited for an interview was Robert Noyce. Noyce was so assured of being offered a job that on arriving in Palo Alto he immediately found a house to rent near Shockley's laboratory – *before* the interview.

Robert Noyce, c1965.

87

It was later that year that Shockley, having assembled his team, was awarded the Nobel Prize for his part in the invention of the transistor. The future of Shockley Semiconductors seemed sealed. But while the company's outward appearance was upbeat, deep currents of frustration

Brattain, Bardeen and Shockley, coinventors of the transistor.

were running through the engineering staff.

Shockley's genius at invention was not matched by his managerial skills. Distrustful and arrogant, within a year he alienated almost everyone who worked for him. In 1958, a group of Shockley's engineers, including Bob Noyce, Gordon Moore and Jean Hoerni, left to start their own company, Fairchild Semiconductors. The move was a land-mark decision. From these eight men would spring many of the companies that today make northern California's 'Silicon Valley' the centre of the world's electronic business. An embittered Shockley would later call them 'the traitorous eight'.

The eight knew little more than Shockley about running a business. The concept of a start-up company did not exist. The firm survived initially by making standard transistors, always looking to make their mark. Foremost on Bob Noyce's mind was the 'tyranny of numbers'.

A thousand miles to the southeast, another young engineer, Jack Kilby, who had just started at Texas Instruments (TI), was pre-occupied by the tyranny of numbers. Like Fairchild, Texas Instruments gave high priority to solving the problems it posed. Each of the armed forces was eager to support companies that could help it build complex, reliable, miniaturized electronic devices. Because Kilby had not been with TI long enough to take a holiday he was working during its summer break. It was then that he hit on a brilliant idea. Like Dummer, he saw that the solution lay in trying to make the entire circuit out of one block of a semi-conducting material like silicon or germanium. There would be no wires, no soldering and best of all, it might be possible to make the whole circuit all at once.

To many this seemed a crazy idea. Traditionally, each of the different types of components in electrical circuits was made of the specific material that worked best for that application. Resistors were usually made of carbon, and capacitors out of metal and some insulating material. Silicon and germanium on their own made neither good resistors nor capacitors and were expensive. Undeterred, by the time his colleagues returned from vacation Kilby had designed a device that would herald a new era in electronics.

Later called an integrated circuit (IC)[2] it was the first device that made all the components of an electric circuit out of one basic material. While Kilby used germanium in his first device, silicon would quickly become the preferred material. Kilby also knew that, in theory, it ought to be possible to make all the electrical connections between the different components in one step. In practice, however, he could not see how to do so because standard transistors of the kind he was using, were bulky and shaped like tiny mesas. The ridges of the mesas produced an uneven surface which ruined many connections.

Back in Silicon Valley, the scientists at Fairchild had found an answer. One of the original eight, Jean Hoerni, invented a way to make

89

The eight founders of Fairchild Semiconductors. Gordon Moore (far left), Robert Noyce (fourth from left) and Jean Hoerni (second from right).

transistors flat. Instead of stacking the layers of the transistor on top of each other, Hoerni embedded each layer within the previous one. This was called the planar or flat technique. Once they had made flat transistors the Fairchild scientists started making other flat components like capacitors. Then, unaware of Kilby's invention, Noyce independently hit on the mono-

lithic concept – the idea that all the components could be made out of the same basic material. Noyce realized that it would be technically possible to build an entire flat circuit in silicon and integrate the connections between the components into the structure of the host material.

Here was a complete solution to the tyranny of numbers. Not

only was each component part of the same micro-structure, but all of the connections would be laid down at the same time. The barrier to the advance of electronics in general, and digital computers in particular, had been broken.

But when Texas Instruments and Fairchild both announced the integrated circuit (IC) in 1959, few outside the semiconductor industry understood its importance. And when they were offered for sale two years later, some said the IC's most impressive feature was its high price. A circuit consisting of a few silicon transistors, diodes and resistors cost $120. The same circuit could be assembled more cheaply by hand even after paying for labour. It was more than the commercial market would bear.

Fortunately for Fairchild and TI, events on the other side of the world would change this perception. The Russian Sputnik, the first man-made satellite to orbit the earth, launched in 1957, had left Americans feeling insecure. Facing sharp criticism at home and a public relations nightmare around the globe, in 1961 President John Kennedy seized the

initiative: 'I believe that this nation should commit itself, by the end of the decade [to] sending a man to the moon and returning him safely to Earth.'

As NASA scientists examined what was needed to place a man on the moon, it became clear that to leave and enter the lunar orbit, a spaceship would need to have its own computer on board. Computers at that time (even transistorized ones) filled a room and were too large to fit in a space craft. But a computer built with integrated circuits might be small enough. Also, ICs did not require much power and were reliable.

The moon mission was the boost the new IC makers needed. Here finally, was a need that only they could fill, whatever the cost of integrated circuits. Because of the magnitude of the project and the money it brought, companies were able to start making ICs in large quantities, and their cost dropped.

Another boost came from a contract to build ICs for the guidance computers in weapons systems like the Minuteman II. As the new silicon prospectors made more ICs, they discovered that they could make

91

from a wafer had increased six-fold, the fraction of bad circuits fell dramatically.

With smaller ICs, electrons did not have to go as far between components, so computers made of ICs could compute faster. Smaller chips required less power. And best of all, because dozens of ICs could be built on the same wafer, their cost plummeted. Complex integrated circuits, which in 1959 cost more than a thousand dollars, had dropped to less than $10 six years later.

ICs soon became widespread, appearing in Polaris missiles and jet aircraft, radios and microwave ovens. Integrated circuits continued to shrink, but as the patterns on them became thinner than a human hair, contamination again loomed as a serious problem; a problem solved by sterilizing the factories. Today's integrated circuit factories are thousands of times cleaner than any operating theatre. The workers wear masks and the air flow is carefully controlled. With such measures yields of integrated circuits have steadily grown.

Each jump in yield encouraged chip designers to produce

increasingly fine circuit patterns. This meant using smaller transistors and smaller individual ICs (chips), more of which could be made on the same silicon wafer.

Making smaller chips also reduced one of the main production problems – contamination. Dust and other microscopic particles disrupted the intricate patterns of the wafer. By itself, shrinking each circuit and putting more of them on the wafer did not reduce the number of bad circuits. But since the total number of ICs got more sophisticated and powerful ICs. Gordon Moore became famous for a prediction he made in the mid-1960s, which has become known as Moore's Law. He noticed that the number of components on an IC was doubling every year and predicted this trend would continue. This law has proved remarkably accurate. As this book goes to press the number of transistors that can be crammed into a single chip has risen to 4 million.

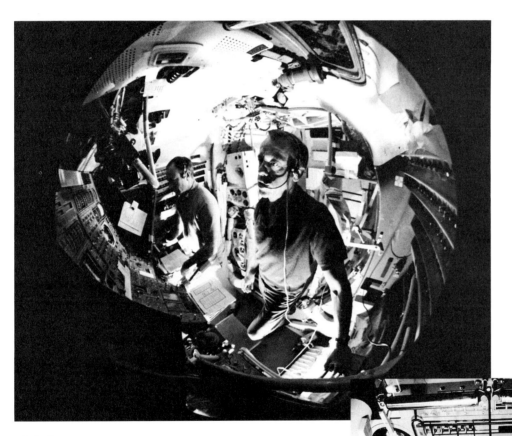

93

Left: Fish-eye view of Complex 37 blockhouse during Apollo 5 countdown. Above: Shepard and Mitchell in the Apollo lunar module simulator.

Right: Interior of Apollo spacecraft showing computer.

In Moore's words:

" If the auto industry had moved at the same speed... as our industry, your car today would cruise comfortably at a million miles an hour, probably get half a million miles per gallon of gasoline. But, it would be cheaper to throw away your Rolls Royce and buy a new one than to park it downtown for the evening. "

As the complexity of chips exploded, so did the population of Silicon Valley. Dozens of small semiconductor companies sprang up, many started by former Fairchild engineers. The Silicon rush was on.

In 1969 a man walked on the moon. The decision to use ICs in the Apollo computer had paid off. Weighing only 54 pounds, the computer was less than one-hundredth the weight of some computers at the time. And unlike other guidance computers, this one did not rely on back-up computers. There was no room for error.

The 1969 moon landing capped a decade of technological achievement. If the IC had made the Apollo mission possible, the moon

project had played a critical role in the development of integrated circuits and the semiconductor industry. In 10 years, the IC had been transformed from an expensive scientific curiosity to the electronic engine that powered not only a wide range of new electronic products but also a growing number of computers.

The low cost of integrated circuits had led to the proliferation of a new type of computer called the minicomputer. Smaller and one-tenth the cost of mainframes, minicomputers offered small businesses the chance to enter the computer age.

Cheap compared to an IBM 360, minicomputers were still expensive. Since one computer might use 10 or 20 special purpose ICs, the cost of a typical minicomputer was about $20 000, still much too dear for the average consumer. But it was easy to see that if trends continued, small, cheap and fast computing would become available to nearly everyone. But few of the mainstream computer companies could imagine why private individuals would want a computer and what they would use it for. Despite advances in hardware, the uses to which computers were put had little changed. Most computer scientists continued to think of the computer as simply an arithmetic and data processing machine.

program ran, the TX-2, was a room-size defence computer, and one of the most powerful computers at the time. The software which ran on it that day harnessed its power in a revolutionary

95

'Sketchpad' on the TX-2 at Lincoln Labs, MIT.

Glimpses of the future

In 1962 at Lincoln Labs[3] – a research centre set up by the Massachusetts Institute of Technology (MIT) – a young graduate student called Ivan Sutherland demonstrated a program called Sketchpad. The machine on which his

way. Sutherland sat in front of a screen and, using a light pen, drew engineering drawings. He did not need to be a skilled draughtsman. If he wanted circles, the computer would draw perfect circles to any scale. He could copy drawings and cut and paste them much as in a modern computer drawing package. It was a new way of talking or *interacting* with a computer and offered a vision of what computers would become.

Sketchpad was one of a handful of projects funded by a far-sighted office in the Department of Defense's Advanced Research Projects Agency (ARPA) headed by J C R Licklider. The office was committed to finding ways of advancing interactive 'real time' computing as a way of achieving a symbiosis between humans and this new machine. But even Licklider was staggered by Sutherland's demonstration. Sutherland had invented the field of computer graphics 20 years early.

To Alan Kay, a talented young computer scientist who would become a prime mover in personal computing, Sutherland's achievement was stunning:

> You can't buy a system today that does all the things that Sketchpad could back then. That's what's really amazing. It had the first system that had a window, first system that had icons, certainly the first system to do all of its interactions through the display itself. And for a small number of people in this community, the Advance Research Projects Agency research community, this system was like seeing a glimpse of heaven. Because it had all of the kinds of things that the computer seemed to promise ...you could ...think of it ...as a light that was sort of showing us the way.

Such demos resonated with gurus like Ted Nelson, a film maker who had stumbled on computers at Harvard University and had gone on to devote himself to telling people what they were really for. Nelson was very surprised that Sketchpad 'did not start a vast movement'.

96

Robert Taylor:
batch processing
'dehumanizing'.

66   In fact, it just stood there as an example that people would gaze at. They'd look at the movie and say, yeah, gee, well that's very inspirational. And they'd go back and do exactly what they were doing, which had nothing to do with interactive computing, because there wasn't any interactive computing. 99

Sketchpad had little immediate impact on the way people used and thought about computers. There were two main reasons for this. Manipulating graphics and text might be easier for humans, but it requires more powerful computers. Few scientists had access to such mighty machines as the TX-2. Then there was the more pressing problem of writing the software itself. The invention of higher level languages like FORTRAN and COBOL had made writing programs easier, but writing complex graphics software was intensely demanding and the programming environment discouraged innovation.

Most computers were anything but interactive. After being written out by hand, programs were prepared on punch cards or tape and brought to a computer centre where they were run in what was called 'batch-mode'. Bob Taylor, a successor to Licklider at ARPA, found batch processing 'dehumanizing':

66   The notion of a human being having to punch holes in lots of cards, keep these cards straight and then take this deck of what might be hundreds and hundreds of cards to a computer and . . .turn this deck over to someone who operates the computer and you go away and you come back the next day and find out that your program executed up until card 433 and then stopped because you left out a comma. So you . . . stake your deck of cards and you go back and you fix that and you go back to the computer again and this time . . .the program got to card 4006 and it stopped because you forgot to punch an O instead of a zero or some other stupid reason. I think it was bleak. 99

If programmers found computers difficult, what chance was there that ordinary people would be able to use them?

97

Towards interactive computing

As computers were prohibitively expensive for individuals to have their own, the big hope for people like Bob Taylor was a scheme called time sharing which had been introduced in the early 1960s. Instead of having one computer based in a computer centre to which programmers brought their jobs to be processed one at a time, time sharing used clever software to allow dozens of people to use the same machine simultaneously. The software instructed the computer to switch between the users so quickly, that users had the illusion that they had exclusive use of the machine. A programmer might type a line, think for a second and type another line or code. In his one-second pause, the computer might have serviced 15 or 20 of his colleagues without him being aware of it. The programmer now interacted directly with the computer and received a response immediately. Programs could be run and mistakes corrected on the spot.

Using time sharing, a young engineer called Doug Engelbart was able to create a remarkable picture of what was to come. Back in the 1950s when computers were still the size of rooms, Engelbart had been struck by a vision that one day ordinary people would sit in front of a computer screen and control it themselves. 'When I first heard about computers, I understood from my radar experience that if these machines can show you information on punched cards and print-outs on paper, they could write or draw that information on a screen.'4 He imagined that people would sit in front of cathode ray screens manipulating text and graphics. Then he set about realizing his dream of 'augmenting the human intellect'.

With funding from the Pentagon's Advanced Research Projects Agency, Engelbart developed a series of ideas and techniques. In 1968, he decided to present his research at the Fall Joint Computer Conference in San Francisco. He did not *tell* his colleagues what he had been up to, he *showed* them in a technological *tour de force*. Linked by microwave television to a computer in the Stanford

Research Institute at Menlo Park in California, he demonstrated a vision of personal computing created by new and powerful software. He worked at a console which had, in addition to a keyboard, a pointing device they had

Doug Engelbart

invented called a mouse (so named because the cord coming out of the back looked like a tail).

Using his mouse, he demonstrated an early word processor, an early hypertext system (an interactive cross-referencing system which

enabled him to jump from document to document) and did some remote collaborative work with his colleagues 30 miles away. In his left hand he expertly used a device called a key set – a shorthand way of sending instructions. It was an inspirational performance for computer scientists like Alan Kay:

> We thought of Douglas as Moses opening the Red Sea. You know he was like a biblical prophet ... they were actually doing the kinds of things that people still dream about today ... I think of it as the vision of what we today call personal computing or desktop computing.

A mild-mannered and modest man, Doug Engelbart hoped his demonstration would convince the computing world to change. Once others saw the true potential of computers, he believed, they would help him to bring it about. But nothing happened. Within the corporate computer business, there was little interest in so-called personal computing. Computers were still expensive and many technical people felt that it was wasteful

99

100

to use them on frills like graphics and friendly interfaces. Engelbart's demonstration, some sceptics pointed out, had cost (by some estimates) over $US100 000 and used tremendous computing power. It seemed ludicrous that such technology should be 'wasted' simply to make computers easy to use.

Other visions of the future fared no better. At the Rand Laboratories in Santa Monica, California, a system for medical workers called the Rand Tablet was shown which enabled users to write on a tablet in ordinary handwriting. The computer would recognize the characters and turn them into typed text. But the invention sparked little interest and was left to gather dust. (Interestingly, character recognition is something many computer companies are researching today.)

Worse was to come. The Department of Defense, which through its ARPA office had been the principal funder for many of these projects, was stretched financially by the war in Vietnam. An amendment passed by Congress in November 1969, cut funds for defence research includ-

ing grants to Doug Engelbart, whose lab was disbanded a few years later.

Meanwhile, the price of computer hardware continued to fall. Gordon Moore's prediction was proving true – every year the cost of computer hardware halved in price and shrunk in size. This meant that the kind of circuitry that Sutherland used in 1962 (the room-sized TX-2 computer) could be delivered in 1970 for about one-two hundred and fiftieth (1/250) of the cost. Projecting 10 years to 1980, it followed that the same circuitry could be bought for about one-two hundred and sixty thousandth (1/260 000) of the cost. So while computers were still expensive in 1970, within a decade they would become much cheaper and more powerful – powerful enough to incorporate complex software like Engelbart's at an affordable price. The computer establishment, however, in Ted Nelson's view, was in the dark.

" Because the establishment never gets it, that's how it is with paradigm shifts. The establishment does not see where the next wave is coming from. And even if they hire somebody to tell them where the next wave is coming from, they never believe them. Which is exactly what happened with Xerox and Xerox PARC. **"**

Xerox PARC

If visions such as Engelbart's failed to win the attention of the corporate computer establishment, they did attract another large corporation – Xerox. Xerox was more than interested, it was frightened. Xerox had built its fortune on xerography, a technology which IBM had decided not to exploit in the 1950s. It involved photocopying large quantities of paper onto even larger quantities of paper. Talk of a paperless future where computers helped move information electronically from desk to desk untouched by human hands, worried Peter McColough, Xerox's chief executive officer.

Xerox, which knew little about computers, did two things. First, they bought an ailing computer company called Scientific Data Systems.[5] Second, in an extraordinary act of foresight, they created the Palo Alto Research Centre – Xerox PARC – to invent the paperless office and explore what McColough called the 'architecture of information'. Having no experience of computer research, they hired Bob Taylor (the former ARPA projects manager) to help them recruit staff. Taylor gathered up the smartest computer scientists he knew, all of whom agreed on the destiny of computers – young scientists like Alan Kay, Larry Tesler, Butler Lampson and Chuck Thacker and many of Engelbart's team – and offered them a challenge – make computers easy enough for ordinary people to use. This group of people would revolutionize the image of computing and implement most of the innovations in personal computing that we take for granted today.

Untidy and informal, the young scientists were misfits at Xerox. As Bob Taylor recalls: 'Computer scientists ... were stereotyped as people who didn't bathe, they didn't shave, they didn't wear shoes, they didn't have any respect for authority.' The PARC scientists did not do things the corporate way. Instead of purchasing a conference table and chairs, Taylor bought bean bags, raising more than a few eyebrows at headquarters. 'Until we pointed out that a conference chair might cost several hundred dollars each, and a bean bag cost $35 and we didn't need a conference table. So there economics carried the day.'

Xerox had agreed to fund them for 10 years to investigate the 'architecture of information'. For most of the scientists like Larry Tesler, their objective was clear.

Xerox PARC, Palo Alto, California.

" We felt that this would be an opportunity to bring com- puting to everyone ... Remember, a computer at that time was thought of as something that was very for- bidding, difficult, highly tech- nological, you had to be a real expert and a doctorate to understand. That was kind of the public image. We somehow had to humanize com- puters and make them a common object that anyone could use. "

The term often discussed was 'user interface'; how to make the computer easy and natural for people to inter- face or interact with. But could a bunch of brilliant, well-meaning scien- tists really make a computer easy for ordinary people to use? Would it suit the office workers Peter McColough had in mind?

Alan Kay believed they could if they took a fresh approach taking their inspiration not from the world of computer science but from children. One of Kay's mentors, the MIT computer scientist and educator Seymour Papert, had studied with the Swiss psychologist Jean Piaget for five years before developing a pro- gramming language for children called LOGO. In Papert's words, children 'give us a window into the way the mind really works, because they're open ... I think we understand ourselves best by looking at children'. Piaget's experiments looked through that window and revealed that children go through stages in which different mentalities are dominant. First, they spend a lot of time grabbing and touching, then visual things become dominant and only later in their teens are they comfortable with so-called symbolic reasoning.

One of Piaget's most famous experiments involves asking a child of about five to pour the same amount of milk or water into two identical glasses. The child is asked: 'Do the two glasses both have the same amount of milk?' He says yes. Then the investigator takes one of the glasses and pours the contents into a tall, very thin glass. While the thin glass contains the same amount of milk, it rises to a higher level than the milk in the other glass, and this fools the child. When asked again: 'Do the glasses still have the same amount of milk?', the child now says: 'No. Now this one (the tall thin one) has more.' He says this because his visual men-

tality is dominant, and he does not yet understand 'conservation'.

The American psychologist, Jerome Bruner, and other experts have come to view these mentalities as semi-independent processors in the brain. There are, it seems, separate and equally powerful ways of knowing about the world. These mentalities that can be distinguished in growing children – the kinesthetic (the sensation by which bodily position, weight, muscle tension and movement are perceived), the visual, and the symbolic – remain with them all their lives. If, Kay reasoned, one could use the more intuitive mentalities of touch and vision in designing computers, the machines might become easier to operate.

At the time, most computing was unintuitive. Whereas in real life if a file was wanted, one would simply look to see where it was then reach out and take it; the same operation in a computer involved remembering a set of abstract symbolic instructions. Projects like Engelbart's and Sutherland's had been so appealing exactly because they tapped into these intuitive mentalities. The mouse

103

104

turned out to be the perfect kinesthetic device. It fitted neatly into the hand and with it people could reach out and, by clicking it, select, grab and drag objects on the screen. Kay and Tesler and their colleagues at Xerox PARC also realized that with the right software they could control the bits on a television screen to make a highly flexible and responsive graphical world – a so-called bit-mapped display.[6] By 1972, Kay's group had programmed a simulation of a painter's palette, which resembles many of today's paint programs. By putting together the bits differently one could make elaborate fonts with which to write. Other software could synthesize or transcribe music. Software could conjure up illusion after illusion and, by doing so, change the very nature of the machine. As Tesler puts it:

66

What we realized was that we could create what some people called a user illusion, something that appears to be a *world on a screen*. One way to think about it [is] if you play a video game... there's an illusion of spaceships or roads and cars... and the user who gets engrossed in the game... starts operating as if they're really working in the real world when, when in fact, they're only working in this imaginary, simulated world created by the sequence of steps in the computer program.

99

How would this bring about the office of the future? If software could create a video game or a paint program could it not also create an illusion of an office with folders and documents and filing cabinets? Everyone knew what an office looked like and how it was organized. So instead of having to learn complicated programming commands to open a file or copy it, the user would be given a graphically simulated desk top, so that they could carry on doing what they knew – grabbing and opening files, sending messages, creating and making insertions in text, cutting and pasting.

While Kay, Tesler and others developed software, hardware geniuses like Chuck Thacker and Butler Lampson were building a personal computer on which to use it. Within two years Thacker and Lampson had produced a prototype computer. Called the Alto, it was unlike any other computer. The screen mimicked paper. There were menus, icons and pointers. It had a mouse. By 1973, Xerox had devised many, if not most, of the basic technologies on which today's personal computers rely. Shortly afterwards, they developed laser printing, sophisticated word processors and ways of networking computers. But today no one thinks of Xerox as a computer company. In a tragic string of events Xerox failed to exploit the riches they had built. They fumbled the future.

Unfortunately for the Xerox scientists who had wanted to bring computing to the people, their patron was under intense pressure in the copier business. Threatened by Japanese competition, the management thought that marketing the Alto was too risky. The scientists settled down to perfecting their creation believing that eventually Xerox would come to see sense. But outside the confines of Xerox PARC, things were moving on. Not only were the phenomenal advances in hardware continuing as Gordon Moore had predicted, but the wizards of Silicon Valley had designed another landmark innovation which was to upset the plans of Xerox PARC.

105

*T*he personal computer

In 1968, after 10 years at the helm of Fairchild Semiconductors, the most successful company in Silicon Valley, Bob Noyce and Gordon Moore decided to leave Fairchild and strike out on their own again. By this time, the valley was awash with venture capitalists and they had no trouble either finding sponsors for their new company, Intel, or attracting talent. One of the ablest of their technical team was former Stanford University physics professor Ted Hoff, who would lead Intel to make a contribution to electronics.

In the 1960s the calculator market was fiercely competitive with companies stacking their scientific calculators with complex functions. Calculators more sophisticated than the ENIAC were being sold for a few dollars. One of Hoff's first jobs at Intel was to design a set of 12 integrated circuit chips that would go into a calculator for the Japanese company Busacom.

He came up with a radical idea. Why design 12 special purpose ICs for the Japanese calculator this time, another set for a missile guidance system and yet more for a music synthesizer? Why not put all the circuitry on a single integrated circuit and then, like a normal computer, program it to do whatever you want?

Like a real computer, Hoff's device, called a microprocessor,[1] could be used as the guts of a general purpose machine – a calculator, data processor or music synthesizer, depending on how it was programmed. The program was usually stored permanently in memory chips. So the microprocessor was dubbed a 'computer on a chip'. And just as most people had failed to

Ted Hoff

see the importance of the IC so they failed to grasp the importance of this new development, Busacom included. As Hoff recalls: 'When I told the Japanese engineers what I had come up with they weren't the least bit interested. They said they were out to design calculators and nothing else.'

Intel, however, decided to develop the microprocessor anyway, and by 1970 had built a working model. Although there were problems to iron out, Bob Noyce, the head of Intel, realized that sooner or later the microprocessor was going to revolutionize the computer business. With the guts of the machine on a piece of silicon small enough to fit in your hand, it was only a matter of time before computers would become a lot smaller and cheaper. Then they could be sold in far greater numbers.

But what was clear to Noyce was not clear to the leading computer manufacturers. Many, such as IBM and DEC, considered building small, inexpensive computers based on the new microprocessors, but decided there was no market. They could not imagine why anyone would need or want a small computer; if people wanted to use a computer, they could hook into any of the growing number of time-share systems. It was not only the business executives who failed to spot the microprocessor's potential; many technical types did too. Once when Hoff was asked by one of the latter how he would repair a chip, he replied: 'No it's not like that at all. It's like a light bulb. When it burns out you unplug it and throw it in the garbage and plug in a new one.' Hoff's colleagues were dumbfounded at the idea that a computer could be so cheap you'd think about throwing it away.

While corporate bigwigs shunned the microprocessor and dismissed the idea of small computers, others were wildly enthusiastic. These were the hobbyists, the hackers, the nerds – highly technical people at the margins of society. They did not believe that the computer, the 'neatest toy' to come along, should belong only to the likes of IBM.

Ted Nelson, a guru to these hobbyists, had been trying to awaken America to his vision of computers for 10 years. He despised the corporate computer establishment for appropriating what he saw as the greatest invention since the printed book.

> **They [the computer establishment] could not imagine that anyone besides their trained captive market would be willing to use a computer, or would have any use for a computer, because they knew computer users as these highly disciplined troops who would come in with their problems neatly punched onto cards and would obey all the rules and wait at the window until their print-out came back. And they couldn't imagine any other style of usage such as the person being able to sit down at his or her own computer and wham away at the keyboard and produce pictures.**

Fuelled by Nelson's ideological passions, and the technical magic of nearby Silicon Valley, the grassroots computer movement in the San Francisco Bay area was ready to explode. All it needed was a spark.

That spark would come from a small, struggling calculator company called M-I-T-S, or MITS, tucked in between a massage parlor and laundromat in Albuquerque, New Mexico. In 1974, a price war in the calculator industry was ruining the company and its owner, Ed Roberts, was ready to quit. But in a desperate act of survival, he hatched a wild plan to build a small computer based on one of the new cheap microprocessors, Intel's 8080, and to sell it for the unheard-of price of $500 (some went for as little as $395). Roberts' computer, which he called the Altair (not to be confused with Xerox PARC's Alto), was announced on the cover of *Popular Electronics* magazine in January 1975. The picture on the cover was of a fake; the prototype had been lost in the mail. But the readers did not know that. The day the magazine came out, Roberts received five calls about the microprocessor, the next day nine, and by the end of the week he was getting between 25 and 30 enquiries in a day. Within a month, Roberts had gone from the brink of bankruptcy to having a quarter of a million dollars in the bank.

The Altair was a far cry from Xerox PARC's Alto or any of today's personal computers. It had no keyboard and no screen. It was not even assembled; buyers received a set of parts. No software programs came with it, and the only way to program the machine was to flick the tiny switches on its front panel.

Larry Tesler of Xerox PARC, who went to see the Altair, recalls having mixed feelings. He was fascinated that a computer that people could afford had been built as early as 1975 but 'when it came down to it, we ended up ridiculing it because the user had to assemble the machine... himself'. Still, Tesler recalls that 'it did start to dawn on us that maybe we weren't the only people understanding that personal computing was going to happen.' And it happened faster than anyone thought. Despite all the limitations of the Altair, it satisfied a hunger. In Ted Nelson's words:

109

66

What happened was all this pent-up demand... was allowed to burst forth. It was as though all the galley slaves were suddenly able to jump overboard in life preservers with their own little computers because they were no longer enslaved to the computer center and its bureaucratic mentality.

99

In particular, the Altair ignited the grassroots computer movement around San Francisco. One night in March of that year, a group of computer hobbyists in the area found their way to Gordon French's garage and formed a club that would transform Ed Robert's lightning bolt into the personal computer revolution. The group of 22 hackers called themselves the Homebrew Computer Club.

The group grew rapidly and was soon filling an auditorium at nearby Stanford University. It attracted an eclectic mix of hi-tech hippies, apolitical computer nerds and budding entrepreneurs, all eager to show off their own 'homebrewed' computers. One member was Stephen Wozniak; the club was a turning point:

66

The Homebrew Computer Club was the most important event of my life. I lived for it. Every spare minute of every day, up late till 2, 3, 4 in the morning. I had asthma for a while and couldn't sleep and had to force myself to stay awake. So I wrote programs. I always tried to get the next stage of my computer done by the meeting. And I don't think I ever failed to do so. But boy, it really drove my life, gave it a reason to have a schedule, but that's because it was the most important thing happening in the world. It was like a revolution that I'd never seen. You read about technological revolutions, the Industrial Revolution and here was one of those sort of things happening and I was a part of it.

99

110

These impromptu discussions led Homebrew members to form dozens of small companies which built add-on devices for the Altair, such as circuit boards to increase the computer's memory. Initially this entrepreneurial activity had little effect on the free flow of information at the Homebrew meetings.

company formed by Bob Marsh and Lee Felsenstein called Processor Technology. Off in a corner of the hall, far away from all the excitement, was a group of unkempt men selling circuit boards off a card table. Two of them would become synonymous with the personal computer – Steve Jobs and Stephen Wozniak.

Other computer hobbyists in Boston, Chicago and Trenton, New Jersey, also formed clubs. One hot weekend in August 1976, these pioneers converged on New Jersey's Atlantic City for their first convention. The big movers at the time were Ed Roberts' MITS and a

As young teenagers growing up in Silicon Valley, Wozniak ('Woz') and Jobs had developed reputations as hi-tech pranksters. In the early 1970s they had built and sold so-called 'blue boxes' to make free telephone calls. Inspired by the Homebrew Club, Woz had built a rudimentary computer on

Left: Meeting of Homebrew Computer Club.
Above: Lee Feisenstein, founder member of the Homebrew Club at a club meet.

a circuit board. On Jobs' suggestion, he called it the Apple I. As Woz recalls:

> " I was not designing a computer with any idea we'd ever start a company, ever have a product, ever be successful. It was just to go down to the club and show off, and to own and to use. Steve started coming up with ideas right away, about how this thing could be turned into product, how it could be marketed. And he knew that I was a great designer and so he kind of stayed on top of it. "

Operating out of the garage of Jobs' parents, they gathered together enough parts and money to make a few dozen circuit boards for the Apple I. By 1976, at the Atlantic City convention, where companies like MITS and Processor Technology were selling complete computers, all Jobs and Woz had to show were a few circuit boards. But not for long. They were a formidable pair: Woz, a technical genius, and Jobs, charismatic and very determined.

Jobs rang Intel, the company that had produced the microprocessor, to find out who did their

advertising. Learning that it was a firm called Regis McKenna (after the owner), he set out to persuade Regis McKenna to take them on as well. McKenna was taken aback when Jobs walked into his office:

> " I think Steve had sandals on and cut-offs, Levi cut-offs and a T-shirt and what I call a Ho Chi Minh beard and long hair down his back and... I... sent him up to see my friend, Don Valentine, the venture capitalist, and Don said: 'Why did you send me this renegade from the human race?' "

Valentine referred them to a former engineer from Intel named Mike Markkula. This was their biggest break. At 32 Markkula had retired from Intel a millionaire, and was spending part of his free time helping young entrepreneurs. The pair interested Markkula and he went down to Jobs' garage. He was struck by a new version of their computer called the Apple II: 'I looked at it and I said this is the first affordable useful computer for people. The two guys really didn't have the background and experience to start a company and make it successful. So I agreed to help them.'

Markkula put up $90 000 of his own money and convinced the two Steves to move out of their makeshift factory in Jobs' garage into a warehouse in Silicon Valley. This was the beginning of the Apple empire, which would become a model for all would-be computer entrepreneurs.

With solid money behind them, Woz and Jobs worked feverishly to make the Apple II prototype into a complete computer – a computer that would become an industry standard. Woz designed the Apple to produce colour graphics, one of the first home machines to do so. Apple began to diverge, in product and philosophy, from other hobbyist companies which had grown from the Homebrew culture. Whereas most Homebrew companies were still reacting to the hobby market, Apple, in Markkula's words, 'had a different vision... We wanted to make computers that everybody could use, not just hobbyists.'

This was the same ambition of many of the Xerox computer scientists, stalled in their attempts to persuade the management to sell their Alto computer. Fate would

Homebrew Club, Silicon Gulch Gazettes.

113

bring Apple and Xerox PARC together. But not yet.

Markkula knew that to break out of the hobbyist market the young company would need a solid corporate image and a lot of advertising. So he went to see Regis McKenna and bludgeoned him into accepting them as clients, agreeing to pay personally all the bills for the first three months. Next, Markkula hired experienced engineers and managers from Silicon Valley to run the

114

company, including Apple's first president, Mike Scott.

While Markkula was laying the groundwork, Woz and Jobs worked day and night getting the Apple II ready for its debut in March of 1977 at the second gathering of computer hobbyists – The West Coast Computer Faire. An overflow crowd of thousands waited hours to get into the hall. Once inside they were not disappointed. Hundreds of exhibits showed off the latest computers and applications – proof that the home computer industry had arrived.

With its new wide appeal and easier to use computer, Apple racked up $700 000 in sales in 1977 rising to $7 million in 1978. But they were not alone. Also at the fair were mainstream companies, such as Radio Shack and Commodore, who were introducing computers of their own like the TRS-80 and PETs. Like the Apple II, these machines were simple to use and aimed at the general public. The entry of large, established companies threatened to snatch the industry from the hobbyists and entrepreneurs who had created it.

But what worried Mark-

kula most of all was the prospect that IBM, which had hitherto dismissed personal computing, would come in and crush them all. To survive, Apple had to grow large, and very quickly. They needed to produce something to set their computer apart from the competition. The answer was the floppy disk drive.

One of the main limitations of personal computers at the time was that they stored software programs on ordinary cassette tape, the same kind used to record music. While this was a cheap method of storage, it was undependable and slow. It could take up to five minutes to load a word processing program. Some companies were offering disk drives a hundred times faster than cassette tape. But these were costly and still somewhat unreliable.

At Markkula's urging, Apple developed an affordable, dependable disk drive of their own. Thanks to Woz's brilliant design (his disk drive used just five chips whereas everybody else's needed about 50) they ended up with the best and cheapest disk drive, giving Apple an unassailable position. Another Apple advantage was that the machine had what in those days was a large internal memory (48 kilobytes), which meant it could run longer programs more quickly. But they needed one more break. In all the hardware euphoria, people had almost forgotten that what makes a computer helpful is software, and so far few programs had been developed. Without this software, the personal computer would fail. But in 1979 a superb and novel piece of software called VisiCalc, a financial spreadsheet program, was written by a Harvard Business School student and his friend. It was an instant success, but needed a machine with a reliable floppy disk drive and good memory on which to run. Apple was there.

By some estimates, roughly one-quarter of all Apple computers bought in 1979 and 1980 were purchased by businesses solely to run VisiCalc. VisiCalc proved the usefulness of personal computers. Software programmers flocked to Apple and created an impressive array of applications – word processors, other spreadsheets, educational programs, and of course, games. Wozniak and Jobs realized that their dream of computers for the people was coming true. As Jobs recalls:

> When I saw people that could never possibly design a computer, could never possibly build a hardware kit, could never possibly assemble their own keyboards and monitors, could never even write their own software, using these things, then you knew something very big was going to happen.

Kids with a personal computer.

Right: Child aged 25 months

with Apple II computer.

Apple burst out of the pack. Sales sky-rocketed from $7 million in 1978 to more than $48 million in 1979, and double that again in 1980.

In December of that year, Apple went public in the largest public share offering in 20 years. All of Apple's 4.6 million shares were snatched up within minutes. Apple employees, many of whom had been paid with stock, were suddenly rich beyond their dreams. Jobs, Wozniak and Markkula each ended up with more than $100 million. In total, more than 40 Apple employees and inventors became instant millionaires.

The company's success attracted the media. With Regis McKenna's savvy hand guiding Apple's public relations, the Apple computer became a household name, and Jobs and Woz celebrities. McKenna laughs when he recalls his strategy:

> I used to play this little game. Give me the name of the president of IBM? Give me the name of the president of Texas Instruments? No one can give you those names. Who's the head of Apple Computer? Everybody says, Steve Jobs, right? So it became personal. So the people who ran the company were personal, the products were personal, the culture of the company is personal and it was specifically to contrast ourselves with the history of monolithic, impersonal computing.

While the public's perception of Apple was a company run by two whiz-kids – Jobs and Woz – the truth was that Apple's success was the result of a large group of people, not the least of whom were Mike Scott, Apple's president, and Mike Markkula, who had engineered the company's growth from day one. But Markkula did not mind. 'I didn't start Apple to get public recognition or that wasn't part of my goal. The two Steves are young guys and that was really exciting to them to have the limelight and the recognition for what they'd done.'

In 1981 when the company entered its fifth year, it was riding one of the largest consumer waves in two decades. Radio Shack and Commodore were also making record sales, and Adam Osborne made his fortune with the first portable computer, the Osborne I. In February 1980, the British entrepreneur, Clive

Above: Clive Sinclair

Sinclair, launched the first of his popular home computers, the ZX80. Subsequent models like the ZX81 and Spectrum sold in the hundreds of thousands. But one company was strangely absent.

IBM, which had been content to continue selling large mainframe computers, was finally induced to enter the fray. But Big Blue did it in a very un-IBM way. Proving that an old dog can learn new tricks, IBM adopted many of the methods that had made the Homebrew Club prolific. It published the designs of the IBM PC, so that software developers could write programs for it. In fact, the main program (the operating system) for the PC was produced by Bill Gates, who had developed much of the software for the original Altair computer.

IBM also allowed third-party manufacturers to build hardware devices to work with its PC – an extraordinary move for a company so secretive.

When IBM introduced the IBM PC in 1981 at the uncharacteristically low price of $1365, it signalled to the world that personal computers were the machines of the

117

future. Even Apple welcomed IBM's entry because of the legitimacy it brought to the personal computer market. With the addition of the IBM PC, personal computer sales surged again and sales soon topped the million mark. In 20 years, computers had been brought down to human scale – transformed from huge, mysterious machines to small friendly devices that could be used by children – a transformation made possible by the silicon chip and the pioneering spirit of a group of computer hackers. In 1982 *Time* magazine broke with tradition and instead of putting a Man of the Year on the cover, they named the computer the Machine of the Year.

But the euphoria did not last long. The next year an industry shake-out would start. Adam Osborne would go bankrupt, others would fail. Apple's new computer, the Apple III, was a disaster, and a low-priced IBM PC, the PC Jr, flopped. By late 1983 the personal computer revolution was stumbling. It was stumbling because the personal computer had been oversold: the software was not up to the salespeople's promises. The brilliant software of Xerox PARC had yet to

be revealed. This was about to change. Late that year Steve Jobs addressed his salesmen in Hawaii. Setting the scene for the new product he was about to unveil, he gave them a history lesson in personal computing. After describing the industrial upheaval, he turned to Apple's prospects in a sector increasingly dominated by IBM.

66 It's 1983, Apple and IBM emerge as the industry's strongest competitors. The first major firm goes bankrupt with others tottering on the brink. It is now 1984. It appears IBM wants it all. Apple is perceived to be the only hope to offer IBM a run for its money. Dealers initially welcoming IBM with open arms now fear an IBM dominated and controlled future. They are increasingly and desperately turning back to Apple as the only force that can ensure their future freedom... IBM wants it all and is aiming its guns on its last obstacle to industry control – Apple. Will Big Blue dominate the entire computer industry, the entire information age? Was George Orwell right about 1984? 99

Glimpsing

reality through illusion

It is time to explain what happened back at Xerox, because the product Jobs was to reveal, and on which he was basing his entire company, had much to do with Xerox PARC. Let us return briefly to 1979.

Despite the appeals of its scientists, Xerox had declined to exploit the Alto. But the company which had invented the future, and then ignored it, now did something even more astonishing – they gave it away. Xerox's investment group, whose job it was to put money in new, growing companies sought a stake in Apple. In the negotiations, it was tentatively suggested that a deal be struck with Apple to have them make, at low cost, the computers that PARC had developed. An agreement was made that Steve Jobs and some of his colleagues should visit the PARC research labs.

Larry Tesler, one of the Xerox PARC scientists, recalls that:

" Some of the Xerox scientists were somewhat reluctant to [meet them]. For one thing they assumed that they [the Apple staff] would be a group of poorly-educated hobbyists (i.e. without computer science degrees) who didn't really *get* personal computing. They were pushing these little plastic boxes with hardly any memory out there and couldn't possibly appreciate what we were doing. "

But Steve Jobs appreciated immediately the brilliance and importance of their work. He saw what the Xerox management had not: 'It was just instantly obvious to anyone that this was the way things should be. And so I remember coming back to Apple thinking our . . . future has just changed. This is where we have to go.'

Xerox's tentative plan for Apple to make its computers back-fired. Jobs was to take the PARC vision and try to deliver it at a cost the consumer could afford. Two dreams of personal computing, Apple's and Xerox PARC's, were about to merge. But the process would not be easy. In Jobs' words:

" At Apple what we had to do was two things. One was to complete the research which really was only about 50 per cent complete. And the second was to find a way to implement it at a low enough cost where people would buy it. That was really our challenge. "

Many of the Xerox computer scientists, believing their work would never be commercialized and fearing that time was passing them by, began to leave. Tesler and Kay ended up at Apple. A large group of scientists, especially those interested in computer networking, followed Bob Taylor to DEC.

Alto's technology was expensive, yet personal computers were expected to be cheap – under $2000. Jobs slaved to find a compromise between power and price. Xerox did not, and in 1981, brought out their own computer based on the Alto called the Star. A fabulous machine, with a fabulous price of $16 000, it went largely unnoticed in a crowded personal computer market.

If by now the reader is feeling sorry for Xerox, there is a footnote. Ironically, Xerox did get something out of this affair that paid for their research many times over. In the years ahead the laser printer – another PARC innovation – was hugely successful and put paid to the myth of the paperless office. But PARC's outstanding innovations in personal computing, especially those concerning the user interface, were for someone else to exploit. That person was Steve Jobs.

The quest was tough and nearly broke the company.[1] By the time Jobs addressed his troops in Hawaii, he revealed to them the machine he claimed would change the face of computing. The machine was called the Macintosh and the launch date was set for 23 January 1984. As his talk finished with the words, 'Will Big Blue dominate the entire computer industry, the entire information age ... Was George Orwell right about 1984?' the frenzied crowd shouted 'No,

no, no!' Suddenly the lights dimmed and a short film, a commercial for a new machine called the Macintosh, was shown.

The commercial, which was featured on news programmes around the world, centred on the Orwellian date, 1984, and Big Brother was, although never mentioned by name, IBM. It showed a beautiful athletic woman with a sledge hammer being chased by the 'thought police' towards a hall where hundreds of oppressed workers were listening to a screened image of Big Brother trying to indoctrinate them. She enters the hall and throws her hammer into the screen, shattering it, and releasing a wind – the wind of free personal computing, which awakens the oppressed computer workers. It is a deeply symbolic piece, and only at the end is a computer mentioned: 'On January 23, Apple will introduce the Macintosh and you'll see why 1984 won't be *1984.*'

The advertisement, devised by the Chiat Day company, attracted worldwide attention. At press conferences Jobs and John Sculley, Apple's chief executive

121

officer, proclaimed that a new order had come to computers. They described the Mac as the computer for the rest of us. It was, they said, 'as easy to use as a telephone.' The 1984 commercial was followed by others in which desperate users were depicted trying unsuccessfully to use their unfriendly office computer – usually an IBM compatible. As they worked, manual in hand, the computer beeped 'syntax error'. After a couple of beeps, the user would pick up a chain saw or hammer and demolish the computer, after which the Mac would appear and the message: 'If *you* find computers frustrating, test drive the computer you already know how to use.'

The advertisements were largely hype, but the Macintosh did usher in a new era in computing. Here

122

was a computer simple enough for a child to use. The screen looked like paper; it had icons which could be selected and moved with a mouse. One child born that year was Lara Pullan. Her parents, both accountants, worked at home with Macs so she grew up surrounded by them. When she was 18 months old, her father took an amazing film of his Mac kid. Lara, who at the time could hardly talk, and could not begin to read, climbs on the stool, picks up the mouse, clicks on the hard disk and opens a painting program. She selects drawing tools and makes circles of different shades, saving files as she goes. Even in 1991, most people watching this performance are stunned. No more powerful testimonial to the genius of Xerox PARC can be found.

By comparison, other personal computers were as unfriendly as ever. They were smaller than the IBM 360s but almost no concession was made to the user. There was nothing intuitive about the interface. The user was faced with an ugly black screen covered with abstract symbols. Instead of icons (a picture of a file, say) there were file names, and some-

Apple making PR capital out of IBM's entry into the PC market.

Welcome, IBM.®

Seriously.

Welcome to the most exciting and important marketplace since the computer revolution began 35 years ago.

And congratulations on your first personal computer.

Putting real computer power in the hands of the individual is already improving the way people work, think, learn, communicate and spend their leisure hours.

Computer literacy is fast becoming as fundamental a skill as reading or writing.

When we invented the first personal computer system, we estimated that over 140,000,000 people worldwide could justify the purchase of one, if only they understood its benefits.

Next year alone, we project that well over 1,000,000 will come to that understanding. Over the next decade, the growth of the personal computer will continue in logarithmic leaps.

We look forward to responsible competition in the massive effort to distribute this American technology to the world. And we appreciate the magnitude of your commitment.

Because what we are doing is increasing social capital by enhancing individual productivity.

Welcome to the task. apple

times files were not allowed to have more than eight letters. All operations had to be initiated with obscure commands like 'ERASE A:AUTOEXEC-.BAT', which is the instruction to delete a particular file on disk drive A. (To delete a file on a Mac, the user positioned a pointer on the icon of the file with the mouse, and dragged it into the waste basket for disposal.) A mistake like forgetting to put a disk in the drive would print the error message: 'Not ready error reading drive A; Abort, Retry, Ignore?'

Once it became obvious that non-technical users found Macs much easier to use than other PCs and that there were a large number of potential non-technical users, other computer makers had to develop software to give their computers the Xerox look. It was not the machine itself – the hardware of a typical IBM compatible PC – that was unfriendly but the software which ran on it, particularly the system software.

As the Xerox PARC scientists had realized, software is the science of illusion. The objects we see on the screen – a waste basket, clipboard, a folder – combine to create the illusion of a desk top. This illusion is evoked by millions of lines of code. A simple click on the mouse (to select a file, say) invokes hundreds of instructions in a high-level language – Pascal, for example. When the programmer creates the application program eventually run by the user, each of the Pascal commands gets translated automatically by other software (the compiler) into hundreds of lower level machine instructions that the machine can 'understand'. Ultimately these machine instructions are manifest as patterns of voltages in the machine. So we see that what is to us an object on a screen, is just a mental abstraction: an illusion created on a machine that can carry out a lot of simple switching actions automatically.

As in all illusions, speed is critical. We will wait a few seconds for something to happen, but after that we get bored. Running an applications program (a spread sheet, a graphics program or word processor for example) may involve hundreds of thousands of machine instructions. Fortunately, a modern desk-top computer can perform two million instructions a second. It is thus a paradox of

123

computing that to make things simple for users, the computers themselves (i.e. the hardware) had to become more complex.

With the plentiful, cheap, speedy computer hardware of the mid-1980s, programmers could produce user-friendly software for almost any area of application. Just as software had created the world of the office and word processors, other software enabled the computer to simulate musical worlds, architects' worlds, games and flight simulators. Computers had become universal machines in practice as well as in theory.

Ted Nelson thinks the very name 'computer' is an anachronism:

66

We call them computers because historically we just happened to use them first for numbers. They could have been used for controlling moving signs like baseball scoreboards. In which case we wouldn't have thought of them as numerical. We would have thought of them as textual and graphical machines first and then recognized their numerical functions afterward.

So it's an historical accident that they're called computers and this has misled a lot of people. What they really are is all-purpose machines that can be turned to any purpose by instructing them.

99

The new conjurors

We have seen the power of software to conjure up illusions. This conjuring involves thinking of a series of steps in a procedure which itself can require from hundreds to tens of thousands of instructions. When written out, without mistakes and in the right order, these arcane instructions can make the computer into everyone's dream machine. In the 1960s at centers such as MIT, individuals hooked on programming became known as hackers. By 1980 it was clear that programmers were the key to the future of the personal computer.

At the same Hawaii conference where he introduced the Macintosh, Steve Jobs invited some of the principal software players to participate in a spoof of the American show, *The Dating Game*. Among the programme's guests were Bill Gates and Mitch Kapor, the second of whom had pioneered the spreadsheet program to make Lotus 1–2–3, which has sold over 5 million copies to date.

Having started programming as a youngster, Gates had dropped out of Harvard University to write the interpreter for the Altair and had become a big software name by July 1980, when IBM asked him to write the operating system for their PC. Today, still in his mid-30s, he is worth close to $4 billion.

It is one thing to hack on your own, and another to try to turn software into an industry. In the short history of the commercial software industry its leaders have noticed important differences between building in physical media like concrete, and building edifices of thought in digital electronic media. In a building project that is running behind, one option is to hire more people. In a software project this does not always work. More people can slow it down.

Another difference comes from the immense flexibility of computer instructions, which are much easier to change than reinforced concrete. This very flexibility has become, in Mitch Kapor's view, a liability:

66 In every software project I've ever been involved with there's an overwhelming temptation in the last days to go and to change how it works. You can't do that with a building... If you build a five-storey building and you're a week away from being done, you *can't add* another storey. Yet, in the software, at least at the abstract level, the possibility is there. Programmers say it's just code, I could go in and I could add that routine and we could add that new function. But what they don't take into account are the side effects, the consequences... of changing something. 99

Modern software projects can be massively complex. A graphic example can be seen in the first launch of the American space shuttle Columbia on 10 April 1981. Lift off was delayed for

125

126

two days. The reason? Software. The eight computer programs run on that day contained some half a million lines of code to regulate everything from the life support systems on board to the navigation of the craft. But an error in the software caused a discrepancy between the computers on the shuttle and those in mission control. It was later found that the error had resulted from changes and updates in the systems software over several years. But it was also discovered that even with these errors the problem was not certain to occur. In fact only in one launch in every 67 was this failure possible.

Tracking down a problem in a large software program is not as straightforward as with physical entities like aeroplanes or buildings. With a building, the builder first looks for the cause in the most likely place. If a structure is not holding its weight, he looks to see if the joint is tight, or if the screws are right. He does not in Kapor's words: 'have to go and analyze the whole building'.

66

Software doesn't work like that... If you see a problem... when you attempt to execute a certain command, there is no simple and direct way of knowing which part of the code could have the problem. In some sense it could be almost anywhere. And so the detective problem of hunting down the source of the problem is enormously harder than in physical media because digital media don't obey the same simplifying law of proximity of cause and effect. 99

Another difficulty with software is that it is hard to protect from theft. As all software is codified thought, most commonly stored as patterns of magnetic bits on plastic disks, it is easy to copy – something Bill Gates discovered when his Altair interpreter was copied and passed around by members of the Homebrew Computer Club. Companies have tried to protect their software from thieving users as well as competitors. For lawyers, software presents a new phenomenon. What is it? If it is like a work of authorship, a book or a play, then it is protected under copyright law. But programs are virtual *machines*, they might be patentable. The law is being made on a case-by-case basis, and it is too early to see the consequences.

From machine to medium

As the software industry grew in the 1980s, a subtle and profound change occurred: the computer began to root itself in our culture. For years, largely unsuccessful attempts had been made to put the computer into the classroom and teach children how to program, presumably so they could get jobs in the industry. While everyone seemed to agree that computers were 'the future', no one was quite sure what they were for. The BBC Television series *The Computer Programme* in 1982 induced many schools to buy the BBC micro (made by Acorn) in this optimistic but uncertain spirit. Widespread confusion about computers put many youngsters off. But as the 1980s wore on and as software improved (changing the image and nature of the machines themselves), young children began to discover for themselves what computers were really about.

And it was not pro-gramming. A fascinating insight into children's perceptions of computers was revealed on the American young-ster's programme *Sesame Street*. A teacher asks a group of four-year-olds a simple question – what is a computer for? The answers? 'It's for drawing... I use it to do designs... It's for helping you to learn to read... It's for playing games.'

For a new generation of children who had never known the computer as a room-sized number cruncher, it was simply an object in their world. Like everything else it was defined in terms of what they used it for. How it worked was of no interest. What mattered was what it empow-ered them to do. As the computer mediated between them and activities they enjoyed like drawing, writing and reading, they viewed it as a medium for expression more like a pencil and paper than a machine.

For other children the computer was not a *new* medium of expression, but the only one. At a school in Peabody, Massachusetts, like hundreds the world over, the day starts with buses dropping children off at school. Until recently one of the

127

children would not have been allowed to attend school at all. Matthew Huggins, a highly intelligent seven-year-old, was born with cerebral palsy. While he can see and hear, he is unable to control most of his muscles, and cannot speak. Opening a book or turning its pages is not possible for him. A few years ago Matthew would have been sent to a special school. But now, by taking advantage of the computer's versatility, he is able to go to school with the other children.

The same pages his class-mates turn with their fingers, are scanned into the computer where Matthew effectively turns them by operating a switch with his chin. Matthew can also use the computer to 'talk' via a speech synthesizer to his classmates. The computer can also handle sound and pictures. Matthew has been given a lifeline to a universe of thought and learning previously

*11 Previous page: The first
few notes of Beethoven's
Fifth Symphony coded
in binary.*
*12 Top: Jobs and Wozniak
with printed circuit
board for Apple I.*
*13 Right: Stephen Wozniak
at the keyboard of an
Apple Macintosh
computer.*

14 *Above: Jobs and*

Markkula enjoying the

American Dream.

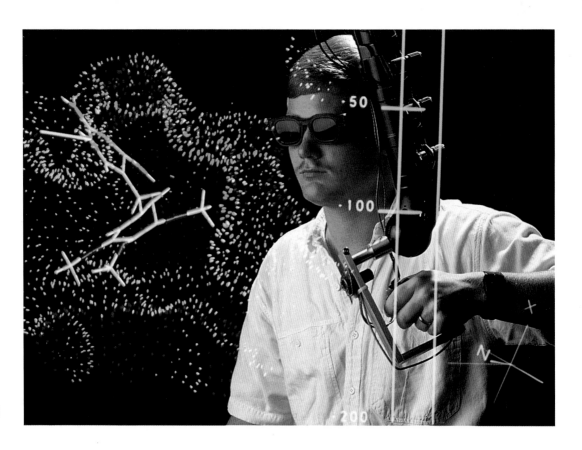

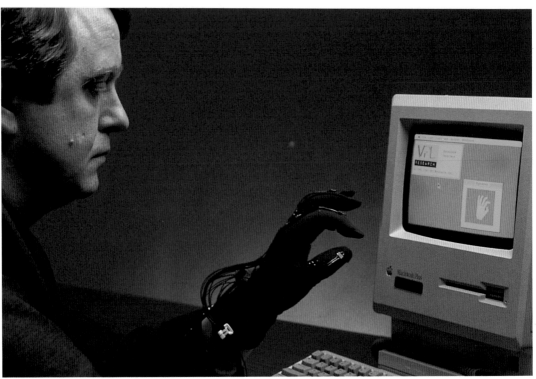

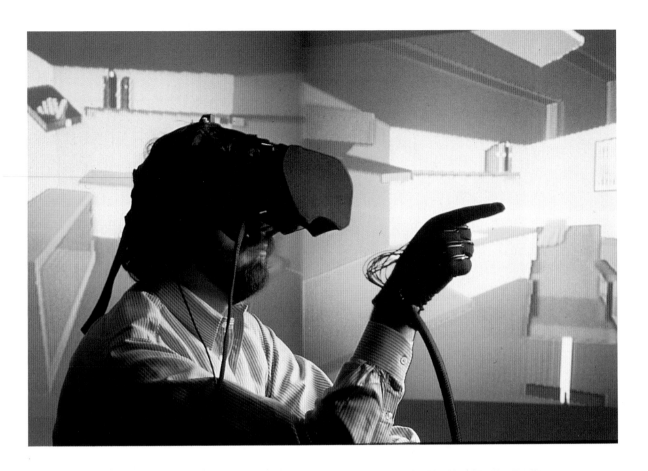

21 *Below: Aerial view of Silicon Valley, California, USA. The area has one of the highest concentrations in the world of semiconductor companies.*

denied him. There are many other children that the traditional medium of literacy has shut out including those who are dyslexic and have problems with reading. These children have one thing in common: the traditional medium for representing ideas – the book – makes those ideas largely unavailable to them. Just as stairs are barriers for children in wheelchairs, so printed materials are a cognitive barrier to children like Matthew. And just as society has built ramps to buildings to allow entry to those in wheelchairs, we can build electronic ramps (computers) into information, self-expression and communication.

Media

For the next few pages we will forget about machines and talk about writing. The invention of writing was one of the most significant events in history.[2] Yet technically, writing is a process of scratching marks on a physical medium. The power in these humble markings lies in what they can represent – knowledge, passions, stories, beliefs, music. They are a way of crystallizing thought, to preserve and communicate it. These markings changed our world: the ideas of one generation could be passed on to the next and influence its attitudes and thought. The marks in a computer

are harder to see, but with a scanning electron microscope and a slowed-down picture they can be visualized. With a computer, numbers, letters and images take on electronic markings. Our ideas are represented as patterns of voltages in the circuits of a machine.

Is the computer an historic event of the same order as the invention of writing? It is too early to tell. What is true is that many of the same misconceptions about computers

Left: Sumarian cuneiform tablet, about 2100 BC.
Right: Egyptian papyrus image, 1310 BC.

129

were held about books. Books are so ingrained in our culture that it is strange to think that they were once viewed as sacred objects. Today, they are widespread and sell for a few pennies second-hand. But in the Middle Ages, illuminated manuscripts, which had to be copied out by hand,

Above: A bookcase in the chained library in Hereford Cathedral.

Below: Chained library, Wimborne Minster.

were every bit as expensive as the early mainframe computers — a single book had the value of a farm.

Scholars wishing to use the books of Hereford Cathedral in England had to secure permission from the priesthood. Three canons with separate keys were needed to open the high security chests where books were kept. Even after printing was introduced, books remained large and expensive. But as in the history of computers, there were visionaries who passionately believed that books should be available to a wider audience. Canon Tiller, the curator of books at Hereford, tells what happened next:

The latest technology which came in at the end of the sixteenth century was the idea of the chained library. Books could be instantly accessible to anyone who visited the library. A book was extracted with the chain just long enough for it to be lowered from the case onto the desk in front of the reader. And there the person could study the book as much as they wanted with no fear of its being removed.

For books to become widespread they had to lose their chains and win the approval of a mass market. The Venetian publisher, Aldus Manutius, is credited with pioneering the portable book, sized so that it would fit into a saddle bag. Portability, better type, affordable prices, writing in the vernacular rather than Latin, more varied subjects, the spread of literacy — all (over five centuries) helped to make the book a popular item; one that was indispensable, yet not precious. Like books, computers have become much smaller and cheaper during their 40-year history. But they are still precious and universities chain them to the desks like their medieval forerunners. Computers, in Alan Kay's opinion, have not found their Aldus Manutius:

" We protect our computers. We bolt them to the desk and so forth... the computer right now is still more noticeable by its presence than its absence. When you go somewhere and somebody doesn't have a computer on them and that becomes a remarkable thing... then I think the computer will have made it. Its destiny is to disappear into our lives like all of the things that we don't think of as technology like wrist-watches, paper and pencils and clothing.[3] "

If the computer does become established as a personal medium, will it bring with it a new definition of literacy? Will students prepare essays on computers involving pictures, sounds and text? Seymour Papert, the computer scientist and educator, puts it like this:

" I think it's perfectly possible that in the future there won't be writing in the sense that we understand it. If literate means putting words on paper with alphabets, I think it's perfectly conceivable that it won't be there except as a curiosity or something that people with a particular attachment to the past like to do. On the other hand, if literacy means being able to access other people's ideas and what's happening in other places, in the past, I'd hope that we'd always be literate in that sense. "

So our paper-based culture may be

131

turned upside down. A new personal medium has the potential to change the very way in which we structure our thoughts.

Completing the illusion – from 2D to 3D

"   I'm in the illusion business. [I] make up illusions for people to help them understand an aspect... of the real world which they did not understand without our illusion.   Fred Brooks, 1990. "

The story is not over yet. Throughout the 1980s, computer graphics, the subject that Ivan Sutherland created with Sketchpad in 1962, grew at a phenomenal rate. Taking advantage of rapidly increasing computer power, master software conjurors created fabulous worlds. Worlds to wow movie goers, worlds to help scientists visualize what is hard to picture. Impressive as they were, they all took place on a flat screen. However convincingly they were rendered they were perceived on a two-dimensional surface. The world we inhabit, however, is three-dimensional.

This limitation had struck Ivan Sutherland by 1965, a few years after producing Sketchpad. It led him to propose a radical idea. What if you could reach through the screen to the simulated world the computer generated and immerse yourself in it. He experimented with a stereo head-up display, two small television monitors in a helmet, and a way of tracking head movements – which gave the user the illusion of being inside a three-dimensional world.

In the late 1960s the technology was barely able to handle a simple geometrical world. It was a vision of something at least 30 years in the future. But Fred Brooks (the IBM scientist who had written the operating system for the IBM 360)[4] was inspired by Sutherland's vision and set up a department at the University of North Carolina (UNC) at Chapel Hill to realize it. Brooks and his team, particularly his colleague Henry Fuchs, have brought this idea to a level where it can be demonstrated – much as Engelbart demonstrated his vision of personal computing in 1968. As in Engelbart's demo, it uses state of the art computing and is immensely expensive. But given the continued advance in hardware performance, this may well be the vision of personal computing in 15 years' time. It is called virtual or artificial reality.

It is a thrilling sight to behold and even more thrilling to experience. A man, Henry Fuchs, puts on a helmet with goggles. The two eye pieces give him a projected view of a computer model of a building. A tracking system in the helmet tracks the movements of his head. If he looks up, he sees what should be above him, if he looks behind him, he sees what he expects to see behind him. He walks on a treadmill which tells the computer where he is in space, and the image is adjusted so that he has the illusion of walking *through* the virtual building. The sensation is hard to describe, and it is unlike any other kind of visualization. The user is *immersed* in a simulated world of thought. He can turn round 360 degrees and look all around him as he moves, as he could in real life. Let Fuchs tell us for himself. He is inside a big hall – a proposed extension to a church – and is admiring the windows and sky lights. Then he starts walking towards a door:

> " In fact, the most interesting part for me is across the hall here to the kitchen. Let me see if I can take you there. You can see there are two doors to the kitchen. I think I'll go through this right one, and we're just about to enter there. … And here we are in the kitchen, and you can see we've got quite a lot of counter space, and quite a few cabinets. In fact, I rather like this nice triple sink. We can walk over to the sink. In fact, just looking at the sink you know, do we want it this way right next to the door here? You could imagine that if I were a member of the building committee, I may recognize something here that I wouldn't recognize as easily in a blueprint. "

During Fuch's 'journey' through the building, he has not moved from a small treadmill. When the real building was built soon afterwards, people who had walked through its virtual counterpart felt they had been there

133

before. To put it another way, two years before a building was actually constructed, people walked through it in their minds. They looked at its columns and gazed at its windows. They grasped the reality of the unbuilt building, experiencing a complex illusion.

In another room at UNC a chemist is standing with a helmet on. In her hand is a small grabbing device (a kind of mouse). She is immersed in a computer model of the room she is in, but there is something else in it – an enormous molecule. She is trying to make a small molecule bind to an enzyme. She is turning and rotating it to fit the cavity, which is the active site. Such a set-up could revolutionize drug design.

Abstractions like large molecules are hard for humans to grasp. Drug design depends on having a good way of representing the molecule so that those with the right properties can be designed to fit binding sites. But in constructing this virtual world Brooks had a problem. While people know all about buildings they have never seen large molecules, except in their minds. Brooks had a

powerful insight – put the molecule inside a virtual room. He recalls:

" We wanted a room-filling molecule. Why? Because it's hard to navigate your way around a big protein. And if you put the C terminus down in this corner of the room and you put the N terminus over in that corner of the room, and you know the room, well you can find your way around in the molecule. It takes on a reality of space that your kinesthetic memory helps you navigate through. "

In future they plan to enrich the illusion using, for example, 'force feedback'. The molecular docking would be accompanied by a sensation of force in the user's hand, based on what is known about real chemical forces. As Brooks is fond of saying, their aim is to grasp reality through illusion. People who are poor at abstract thinking, be it visualizing architectural blueprints, molecules, or scientific theories, will be given another source of access.

The Chapel Hill scientists are bubbling with ideas. They are developing medical aids so that doctors and surgeons can take imaging data from X-rays and other scans and ask the computer to determine the best regime for radiotherapy or surgery and project it over the actual patient. They could then combine what their eyes told them with the computer's mathematical model to ensure their treatment was precise.

A three-dimensional future

The work at Xerox PARC led to the 2D interface, the so-called desktop metaphor, which was highly intuitive. Users could put objects in places on the desktop and leave them there from one day to the next. Virtual reality brings the possibility of 3D metaphors, so instead of the desk top, the whole office. Perhaps office workers of the future will flip down their virtual reality glasses and immerse themselves in a three-dimensional office with a three-dimensional waste basket and filing cabinet. If history is any guide, children of Lara and Matthew's generation will find different uses for it. We can only glimpse how three-dimensional worlds will be used. In Fuch's words:

> Two dimensions... is what we write, it is what we read, it is the pictures we see on the walls. It is the way we communicate with people... The intellectual tradition we have is 2D for the most part. On the other hand 3D is where we live all the time and so even though our professional activity may involve two dimensions, most of the time, our everyday life is three-dimensional. And so I believe that as soon as the computers become capable of being able to interact with the users in three dimensions that the more natural interface would be a 3D one.

135

We can look forward to a future in which the computer will continue the long tradition, which began with writing, of amplifying our intelligence. The visions of Licklider, Engelbart and others, of humans and machines working together, has come to pass.

There have always been, however, those who saw the computer not as a machine to think with, but as an artificial intelligence – a thinking machine. It is to this remarkable story that we now turn.

CHAPTER 7

*T*hinking machines

'We may hope that machines will eventually compete with men in all purely intellectual fields.'   *Alan Turing, 1950.*
'Man has within a single generation found himself sharing the world with a strange new species: the computer . . . Neither history, nor philosophy, nor common sense will tell us how these machines will affect us, for they do not 'work' as did the machines of the Industrial Revolution.'

    Marvin Minsky, 1967

We argued in the last chapter that a computer is a kind of dynamic book, which can manipulate symbols. Yet, this, it seems, is what minds do.

What is a mind? Ask anyone to close their eyes and imagine a house. Ask them what it looks like, how many windows it has, its colour.

Then think about what they are doing. They are manipulating thoughts in their minds in some abstract space, which they perceive as being inside their heads. Taking the experiment further, now ask them to imagine a world with no gravity, so people float in the air. They will have no difficulty obliging, even though these ideas violate natural law. Nor would a computer. As we have seen, a suitably programmed computer can simulate any world we care to describe: one with no gravity; one where time runs backwards; one where left means right and back means front. In both human and computer, the *hardware* – the neurons and valves – *does* obey the laws of physics: if you drop a computer it falls; if a person jumps off a cliff they plunge to the ground, even if they imagine they can fly. But the ideas that human minds and computers represent have no such constraint. Untethered from the hardware on which they run, they can break natural law.

Another mind-like feature of the computer is its 'universality': it can be turned to a vast range of problems. A simulated mind, which only did arithmetic, would not be of

Marvin Minsky with the 'block universe', 1968.

much interest or fun. One which has general capabilities, on the other hand, is irresistible.

It was this line of thought which led a handful of idealistic pioneers in the 1950s to believe that at last there was a way of studying the human mind because they believed a machine had been invented which could be one.

How to build a thinking machine
1. Build a mind

The journey begins, like so many others, with Alan Turing. In

1950 he wrote a paper in the journal *Mind* which began boldly: 'I propose to consider the question, "Can a Machine think?"' In this paper he proposed a test, now generally known as the Turing Test, for determining whether a machine can fulfill the requirement of thinking. The test in its commonly stated form, goes as follows: imagine you are sitting in a room communicating with an entity in another room. The entity could be a person or a machine but is one you cannot see or hear. All communication occurs via a key-board. By asking questions and receiving answers you have to decide if the entity is human.

Unfortunately, Turing, who died in 1954, did not live to see the subsequent development of what became known as Artificial Intelligence (AI). His work was not widely known in America at this time and the subject grew up independently there soon afterwards. But his test stands as a symbol of one of the most remarkable and illuminating intellectual quests of this century – the search for a pure disembodied intelligence.

In 1956, following the New Year holiday, a group of students at Carnegie Tech in Pittsburgh, Pennsylvania, waited for their teacher, the economist Herbert Simon, to begin a seminar on mathematical methods in the social sciences. Among them was Edward Feigenbaum. What happened next, Feigenbaum recalls, had a profound effect on his life: Herb Simon came into class and said: 'Over Christmas, Allen Newell and I invented a thinking machine.'

> " Puzzled looks from students... Machine? Thinking? Thinking Machine? What could that mean? He laid on the table a copy of an instruction manual for the IBM 701 computer. I remember staying up all night, absorbing that manual, undergoing a conversion experience... and then it was obvious what to do for graduate school.[1] "

More precisely Newell and Simon, together with their colleague Cliff Shaw, had sketched out a program for a computer to solve problems in mathematical logic. A few months later they demonstrated a working program called Logic Theorist at a conference at Dartmouth University in New Hampshire, solving problems taken from the bible of mathematical logic *Principia Mathematica* by Bertrand Russell and Alfred North Whitehead.[2] Two scientists from IBM[3], Arthur Samuel and Alex Bernstein, talked about the games programs they were developing. Samuel had been working since 1948 on checkers and Bernstein was engrossed in the longer term task of chess.[4] Marvin Minsky, a young mathematician from Harvard, discussed

Gary Kasparov versus Deep Thought computer chess program, 1989.

the use of computers to prove theorems in Euclidian geometry.

If people who solved hard problems such as these were 'intelligent', were not machines which solved the same problems? One of the conference organizers, John McCarthy, thought so to the extent that he

dubbed the new branch of computer science 'artificial intelligence'. Like Turing, these scientists knew a computer was far more than an adding machine – it was a general processor of symbols. Those symbols (physically represented as patterns of voltages in the machine) *could* stand for numbers, but they might also stand for text, chess moves, pictures, musical notes, or anything one chose. The artificial intelligentsia were full of optimism, for if after a few months, a computer could master tasks as intellectually demanding as mathematical logic or playing chess, this new field had an exhilarating future. Simon, addressing fellow scientists the following year, said: 'It is not my aim to surprise or shock you ... But ... there are now in the world machines that think, that learn, and that create. Moreover, the ability to do these things is going to increase rapidly.'[5]

Simon predicted that within 10 years a digital computer would be the world's chess champion, would discover and prove an important mathematical theorem, and that most psychology theories would take the form of computer programs. Other scientists predicted that soon, computers capable of understanding natural language and of translating text from one language to another would be commonplace.

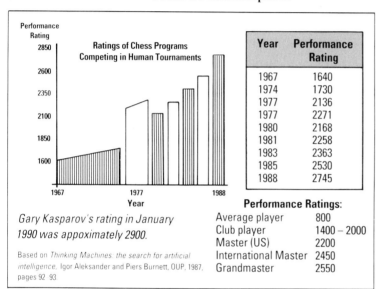

Ratings of Chess Programs Competing in Human Tournaments

Year	Performance Rating
1967	1640
1974	1730
1977	2136
1977	2271
1980	2168
1981	2258
1983	2363
1985	2530
1988	2745

Gary Kasparov's rating in January 1990 was appoximately 2900.

Performance Ratings:

Average player	800
Club player	1400 – 2000
Master (US)	2200
International Master	2450
Grandmaster	2550

Based on *Thinking Machines: the search for artificial intelligence*, Igor Aleksander and Piers Burnett, OUP, 1987, pages 92 93.

Among the pioneers, one would stand out. In 1958 Marvin Minsky moved from Harvard to MIT to co-found with John McCarthy what would become the pre-eminent department in artificial intelligence. He attracted a group of exceptional students and together they began extending the frontiers of computer science. Their work would also have implications for philosophy and psychology. One of Minsky's first recruits was a blind student called Jim Slagle. Slagle embarked on an aud-

acious project. Since everyone was talking about smart machines, what was smarter than solving calculus problems? Slagle set himself the task of writing a program to solve first-year university calculus problems involving symbolic integrals.

Since he could not predict specific questions which would appear, the program had to be smart. Slagle discovered a set of about a hundred rules of thumb (heuristics), and codified them for the computer. While these rules were not guaranteed to work, they could solve most problems. Within two years the computer made an 'A' on the MIT exam. As Minsky recalls: 'It was frightening. The computer was doing as well as the average student or maybe slightly better.'

As news of these activities travelled outside computer circles, a group of people, who had previously

Right: Kasparov against Deep Thought which won the World Computer Chess Championship, 1989.

shown no interest in computers, took note. One such person was Hubert Dreyfus, a young philosophy professor at MIT.

Some of Dreyfus' students who had been exposed to the new science of AI, started coming to his class claiming that they now knew all the answers in philosophy as well as science. According to Dreyfus, 'Students would come into my courses on Heidegger and Wittgenstein, and say, "you philosophers have had your 2000 years and you haven't come up with much, but we are beginning . . . in fact, we've already practically finished understanding perception and particularly intelligence, reasoning and so forth, and in effect, the ball has passed to us." And I was amazed.'

Dreyfus was to devote his career to the philosophical implications of artificial intelligence. Provoked by the students, he began to study the field, becoming a critic of it. But initially, he had to admit that their logic was quite plausible – it was, after all, what philosophers had been trying to do for thousands of years.

The basic AI philosophy went like this: these computers, which

most computer scientists thought were just number crunchers and which the press called 'electronic brains' were neither. They were not brains nor were they simple calculators. They were mind-like machines, which could, in addition to many other things, calculate. Very little was known about how the brain worked but it was obviously different in construction to a computer. The brain had billions of neurons that were highly interconnected. The computer, on the other hand, was made up of thousands of valves laid out with a very definite architecture, executing instructions in a serial, step by step way. Both brains and computers, however, could manipulate 'concepts', therefore both were in some sense minds. The computer (so the argument went) circumvented the need to understand the enormous complexity of the human brain. One could in effect use the computer to study thinking and thereby investigate the laws of thought.

Some of the pioneers of artificial flight had tried to make

Hubert L Dreyfus

141

planes like birds with flapping wings. But, as anyone who has seen the old films of these 'Ornithopters' knows, they were not successful. The biology of birds turned out to be essentially

What made this particularly interesting to a philosopher like Dreyfus, was all this talk of a pure disembodied intelligence. A philosophical tradition stretching back to Plato had argued that one could treat

142

Ornithopters: Far left: Viennese attempt, c1811. Centre: London, 1851 (inventor crashed and was killed). Right: plans from c1795.

irrelevant to making planes. The engineers simply did it a different way, bypassing biology and evolution to make planes with motors. Both birds and planes embody the principles of flight, but those principles are implemented on very different hardware (or featherware). Similarly, the pioneers of AI argued, it does not matter at all how the brain makes intelligence. It is not necessary to copy the brain to make a thinking machine, any more than it is necessary to copy birds to make something that flies. It is the principles of intelligent thought which matter.

man's rational self as separate from the body, for this rationality was what was unique and most noble in us. Our education was and is still based on the idea that to be smart we have to have a trained mind which can reason well. It is this ability to reason which distinguishes us from other life forms. If, as the artificial intelligentsia claimed, they had captured intelligence in a machine then this had enormous philosophical implications.

But had they? As Dreyfus began research for his first book on AI, Minsky and his team were trying to make a computer interact with its environment by giving it a hand and an eye. Connecting the computer to a television camera and a robot arm with a gripper, they tried to program the computer to manipulate blocks. Having succeeded better than their wildest dreams with college calculus, they were now attempting to reproduce the skills of a two-year-old child.

conditions, and is not confused by shadows. A computer, however, has great difficulty in differentiating the block from the space around it. It has to look laboriously for features like sudden changes in image contrast to guide it to the vertices. If the light on two sides of the block has the same intensity, the computer cannot 'see' the edge at all.

143

wildest dreams with college calculus, they were now attempting to reproduce the skills of a two-year-old child.

The task was daunting. Putting the pictures into the computer was easy, but as Minsky recalls, enabling the computer to interpret those pictures was a painful business. A child of two has no problem identifying the edges of the block. He or she can see blocks in all lighting

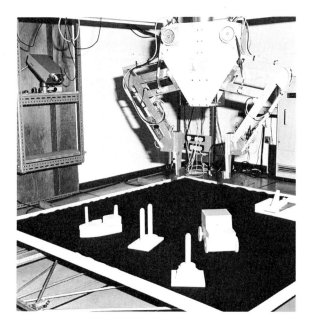

Freddy the robot and blocks.

144

Beyond these problems of machine vision were those of ontology. The machine knew nothing about its tiny world. Minsky recalls: 'We asked the robot to build a tower of blocks and guess what it did? It started with the top block and put it there in space and let it go because the machine didn't know that if you let go of something it would fall. It didn't know about gravity, it didn't know what every two-year-old knows.'[6]

In Britain at the University of Edinburgh they were faring no better. In 1971, a BBC *Horizon* programme on artificial intelligence with the provocative title 'Mind the Machine' visited Edinburgh, then home of one of the leading AI departments in the world, and filmed a robot called Freddy. Like the MIT hand-eye project, Freddy was simply a camera connected to a computer. His world consisted of a dozen objects including cups and glasses placed on a circular piece of white card which revolved continuously. The robot had to look at an object, analyze the picture to distinguish the shadows and the background from the object, and identify which of the 12 items it was watching. To recognize a cup took Freddy over 10 minutes.

Parallel processing

Conventional computers work in a step-wise way – one instruction is performed after another. Electronic speeds disguise this killingly pedestrian way of working. When the calculations are complex or the amount of data to be processed is large (in image processing, for example) the limitations of serial processing by one central processor show up – the time taken to produce results becomes unacceptably long.

The time taken to solve problems can be dramatically reduced if the task is shared between many small processors working on bits of the problem, or on small pieces of the data, at the same time. Simultaneous operation of this kind is called parallel processing. One of the largest parallel computers built is called the Connection Machine which incorporates 65 536 separate processors. Each processor is simpler than those found in ordinary desktop computers but, working together, speeds of 5–10 billion calculations per second have been achieved. The Connection Machine is being used for computation-intensive problems which include modelling fluid flow, image processing and weather forecasting.

Moving and seeing at the same time was more taxing for a computer. At California's Stanford University in the early 1970s, a researcher called Hans Moravec tried to program his CART – a mobile robot connected to a massive computing engine – to cross a 30-metre space avoiding objects. Moravec took films of the ordeal which stand as classic documents of his Herculean efforts. They show the CART's pathetic attempts to cross a room a metre at a time. The film flashes, marking a 15-minute stop (edited out) in which the computer was forced to do some intense image processing (which tied up all of the department's computing power) to determine its next move. A successful run across a 30-metre room involved some 25 of these stops and would take about five hours. Many of the runs flopped or the CART crashed into a chair it had been asked to avoid.

The failure of these robotics programs produced a stunning revelation. The computer had been able to solve difficult calculus problems, but could not cross a room. What did this mean? Was it simply a question of computing power – that the digital computer with its serial architecture simply could not process visual information fast enough, or was the matter more fundamental?

Turing had suspected that the computational problems of vision would be so large that computers would not be able to handle them for many years. His test is phrased to permit a more abstract intelligence without legs, arms or sight. People blind from birth are intelligent and yet they do not see. Paralyzed people are intelligent and yet they do not feel. Without vision and touch, could computers be made to converse intelligently, so they could pass the Turing Test?

The failure of machine-vision *per se* was no reason to give up. Just as Plato had carved off intelligence from the rest of human life and from the body, the artificial intelligentsia could focus on pure intelligence. To pass the Turing Test, however, even a pure artificial intelligence would need to communicate, and this meant being able to use and understand natural language.

145

146

Language

Work on language was active at MIT and elsewhere in the 1960s. Joseph Weizenbaum a computer scientist at MIT, devised a program called ELIZA which sought to reproduce the conversational skills of a Rogerian psychotherapist. It was one of the earliest candidates for passing the Turing Test, and looked, at first sight, as impressive as the Logic Theorist and chess programs. Here is a typical exchange between a human being and ELIZA.

WOMAN: Men are all alike.

ELIZA: In what way?

WOMAN: They are always bugging us about something or other.

ELIZA: Can you think of a specific example?

WOMAN: Well, my boyfriend made me come here.

ELIZA: Your boyfriend made you come here?

WOMAN: He says I am depressed much of the time.

ELIZA: I am sorry to hear that you are depressed.

WOMAN: It's true. I am unhappy.

ELIZA: Do you think that coming here will help you to be happy?

Although ELIZA seems to understand the words, the program is actually based on a series of tricks, ELIZA understands nothing about the meaning behind the words, and often just turns a reply into another question.

WOMAN: Well, my boyfriend made me come here.

ELIZA: Your boyfriend made you come here?

It is also geared to look out for important words like mother, father or dreams. Then it will respond more aggressively.

WOMAN: I have been having bad dreams lately.

ELIZA: Tell me more about your dreams.

Once you realize this it can easily be fooled.

WOMAN: It has come to my attention that necessity is the mother of invention.

ELIZA: Tell me more about your family.

These early attempts to program computers to use natural language revealed something astonishing: that understanding sentences is far more difficult than solving calculus problems. Take a simple sentence like: 'Mary saw the bicycle in the store window, and she wanted it.' While most of us instantly understand what is meant, the sentence is ambiguous. 'It' might refer to the bicycle, the store window or the store, and the correct reference depends not so much on English as on our common-sense knowledge of what people want. In general people want bicycles not store windows. The sentence 'Mary saw the bicycle through the store window: she looked at it longingly and pressed her nose up against *it*' offers more ambiguity. The second 'it' probably refers to the store window and not the bicycle. Interpreting this sentence depends on knowing human anatomy and that people like to be near things that they want even if they cannot have them.

Enabling computers to 'understand' language was to prove more difficult than anyone had imagined. One of the first applications of the digital computer outside arithmetic had, in fact, been language translation. Following the British use of Colossus to break German codes, it was reasoned that if a computer could break a code it could translate (decode) a language like Russian. The idea found immediate favour with the US Defense Department, who were keen to keep a close watch on the Soviets. Human translators could not cope with the proliferation of material in Soviet journals. Millions of dollars were provided, research groups in the United States and Britain were formed, and vastly exaggerated claims followed. Just as the computer had been the solution to the post-war economic expansion, so, some argued, the computer would solve the translation problem.[7]

Soon scientists realized they had underestimated the job. By 1954, Harvard's Anthony Oettinger, head of one Pentagon-funded project, managed to write a computer program to do a word by word translation from Russian into English. But his computerized dictionary was quickly overpowered by the inherent ambiguity of language. The following technical

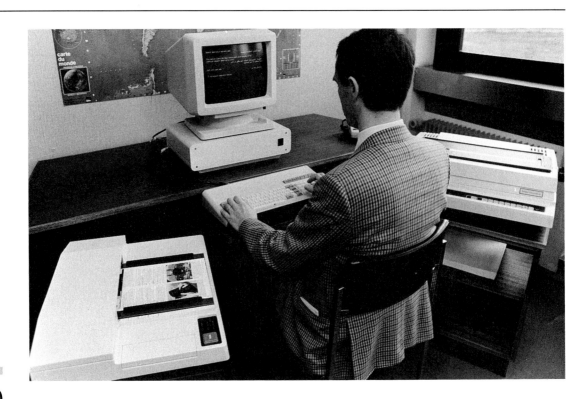

148

phrase translated by a human translator as:

> In recent times Boolean algebra has been successfully employed in the analysis of relay networks of the series-parallel type.

The computer could only produce the following mess:

> (In, At, To, For, On) (last, latter, new, latest, lowest, worst) (time, tense) for analysis and synthesis relay-contact electrical (circuit, diagram, scheme) parallel- (series, successive, consecutive, consistent) (connections, junction, combination) (with, from) (success, luck) (to be utilized, to be taken advantage of) apparatus Boolean algebra.

Even working in the narrow confines of technical literature, the computer's copy needed so much human correction and interpretation that it was not cost effective. The idea of a computer translating *Anna Karenina* seemed impossible. Nevertheless, hype abounded and as late as 1963, on a

Left: Language translator,
SYSTRAN, translates
English into Arabic.
Right: Jean Gachot who
developed the SYSTRAN
language translator.

BBC Television documentary, a spokesman for the National Physical Laboratory's Language Translation Project, predicted that human technical translators would be superseded by computers within 5 years. He was wrong. Despite a great deal of effort, minimal improvement was made and support for machine translation research virtually dried up.[8]

The failure of machine translation showed that language encoded a vast body of shared knowledge. Humans all over the globe, even though they had never met, and spoke different languages, shared a knowledge of what human beings strive for, their beliefs, sensitivities and fears. Knowledge of love and death, humour and despair, knowledge of the many contexts in which human beings find themselves, was common to all. Before

just how difficult the task was. Imagine the problems an alien from outer space would have understanding the following newspaper headlines collected by the Columbia University School of Journalism:

More silverware stolen – police seek pattern

Sharon to press suit in Israel

British left waffles on Falkland

they could translate languages, machines would have to know these things too.

We are so good at understanding language that before computers came along we never realized

The first 15 years of AI had turned the conventional definitions of intelligence upside down. In Minsky's words:

> The things that people think are hard are actually rather easy and the things that people think are easy are very hard. We could do the calculus with just a few hundred pieces of knowledge but to learn language, to recognize

150

faces, to walk and to put your clothes on and do the kinds of things we expect every child to do, we still can't do with the robots and the AIs of 1990.

,,

AI had regressed: starting with college calculus, stumbling on children's stories and stumped with stacking blocks. AI funding began to look insecure. The US Department of Defense was becoming sceptical, and in Britain, the only other country to mount a big effort in AI, the Science Research Council asked the distinguished mathematician, Sir James Lighthill, to review progress. In 1972 he published a devastating attack which all but killed off the British programme. In Lighthill's opinion, the first 20 years of AI research had been a great disappointment. 'In no part of the field have the discoveries made so far produced the major impact that was then promised.'[9]

That same year Dreyfus published his book *What Computers Can't Do: A Critique of Artificial Reason*[10] cataloguing some of the failures. Minsky and his colleagues were undeterred. They focused on machine learning and how to represent knowledge in computers so machines could use language intelligently. The task was overwhelming. To better understand the general problem, researchers constructed special highly-simplified microworlds within which computers might use language intelligently. One of Minsky's students, Terry Winograd, wrote a program called SHRDLU, an imaginary simulated world of blocks which could be stacked in various ways. Using ordinary English, SHRDLU answered questions and carried out instructions in the simulated blocks world.

''

QUESTION: Find a block which is taller than the one you are holding and put in the box.

SHRDLU: By it I assume you mean the block which is taller than the one I am holding?
OK

QUESTION: What does the box contain?

SHRDLU: The blue pyramid and the blue box.

QUESTION: What is the pyramid supported by?

SHRDLU: The box.

,,

UNDERSTANDING A BLOCK WORLD

Let us suppose that we wish to devise a program that will allow a computer to discuss the contents of this block world with a human operator and to control a robot arm that will manipulate the various objects it contains. The first step is to label the seven objects, A–G, and to number the five squares upon which they can be placed. We can now construct a database that describes the existing situation:

Object	Type	Size	Colour	Current Position	On Top Of Object	Under Object
A	BLOCK	BIG	BLUE	1	—	—
B	PYRAMID	SMALL	YELLOW	2	—	—
C	BLOCK	BIG	RED	3	—	D
D	PYRAMID	SMALL	RED	3	C	—
E	BLOCK	SMALL	RED	4	—	F
F	PYRAMID	SMALL	YELLOW	4	E	—
G	PYRAMID	BIG	YELLOW	5	—	—

Describing the shape, size colour and position of each block helps to define a language in which a dialogue can take place with the computer. The computer can respond to questions about the block world. We can ask, for example, 'Is the grey block to the left of the big striped pyramid?' and the language allows the computer to reply. If we instruct the system to 'Pick up the small yellow pyramid', the computer can ask 'Which small yellow pyramid do you mean?

Based on *How Computers Play Chess*, David Levy & Monty Newborn, W H Freeman and Co., 1991, pages 4–5.

SHRDLU could use language unambiguously, but the price was high – you could only discuss coloured blocks. While the AI community saw this as a mild triumph, scientists outside were unimpressed. In this dark period, AI's image would be partially restored by an insight that microworlds could prove useful and profitable.

Edward Feigenbaum, the student who had decided that morning in 1956 to devote his life to AI, was by now working at Stanford University. Feigenbaum speculated that while everyday general intelligence might be hugely complex, perhaps the intelligence displayed by experts – scientists and other specialists – could be captured. In collaboration with the American geneticist and Nobel laureate, Joshua Lederberg, Feigenbaum aimed to devise a computer program to infer three-dimensional chemical structure from mass spectrograph data used by physical chemists.

DENDRAL was the first in a class of programs called expert systems and it sought to reproduce the performance of an expert in a small branch of organic chemistry. It had no pretensions of generality. A few years later DENDRAL was followed by MYCIN, the work of Stanford researcher, Edward Shortliffe, and his colleagues. In MYCIN, an extensive knowledge of bacterial infections was distilled into several hundred rules. The system aimed to capture the dynamic expertise of an area of medicine incorporating rules of thumb and heuristics which a doctor learned over a long clinical career.

The methods Feigenbaum and his colleagues used were similar to those developed in the first 10 years of AI. What was new was an insight of where the power of the expertise lay. The ability to reason was not what made these experts smart in Feigenbaum's view, but the facts and tricks which they knew and others did not:

66 ━━━━━━━━━━━━━━━

[It was] much more important to be knowledgeable about your field than to be clever about your reasoning. If someone here at Stanford was ill, we would run that person over to the Stanford Hospital, because we would find doctors there who were knowledgeable about medicine. Years of training in medical school, internship, residency, experience in the field. We would not run that person over to the Stanford mathematics department, wherein we would find some of the great reasoners in the world. Because reasoning alone won't do. Knowledge is where it's at.

━━━━━━━━━━━━━━━ 99

Dozens of other expert systems began to appear. What was surprising was how narrow an expert's knowledge usually was. In Feigenbaum's words:

66 ━━━━━━━━━━━━━━━

Almost never is an expert system larger than a few thousand pieces of knowledge... Experts are often shocked and startled to find out that in the end it amounted to a few hundred rules. 'Is that all I learned? Is that what I'm doing every day? I'm really exercising just a few hundred rules?'

━━━━━━━━━━━━━━━ 99

153

154

There were all sorts of real micro-worlds of more practical interest than those of coloured blocks; from blood chemistry to geology. But while expert systems helped to save AI from extinction, they had not significantly advanced the quest for a general-purpose intelligence. Expert systems were useful, but they were brittle: when they exceeded their narrow area of knowledge they broke.

Stories of brittleness abound in AI circles. An expert system for approving automobile loans granted a loan to a person who stated on the application that he had spent *20* years in the same job, and was only *19* years old. Doug Lenat, a young American researcher, played a joke on a French expert system for skin disease diagnosis telling it about his 1980 Chevrolet.

> The program asked questions like: 'Are there spots on the body?' and I said yes. 'What colour spots?' Reddish-brown. 'How old is the patient?' Ten years old. And it eventually said the child has measles.

In Dreyfus' words:

> [MYCIN could] tell you what kind of, say, meningitis you have... with more reliability than your family doctor... But if you ask it what a germ is, it doesn't have the slightest idea. Or what is a patient? Or do people prefer to live or die?... then it breaks down. That's the brittleness.

They were like *idiot savants*. An *idiot savant* is someone who is brilliantly gifted in one small area, but outside that area, he is unable to function competently. A fascinating BBC documentary *QED: The Foolish Wise Ones* featured a series of *idiot savants*. One was David Kidd. Give David any date, past present or future and within seconds, he will tell you what day of the week it corresponds to. Outside this narrow area he is learning disabled. When asked to add 8 and 7 on the same programme he gave the wrong answer.

Generally, human intelligence involves a broad model of the world, enabling us to cope with all kinds of situations. To capture it in a computer, scientists had to study not experts with their deep and narrow knowledge, but *children* who excel in knowledge which is broad and shallow.

Common sense

While Feigenbaum developed AI into a business proposition, language researchers at MIT and elsewhere struggled with the task of representing knowledge so that machines could understand the language of simple children's stories. They had realized that the problem was not what the story said, but the huge number of things it left unsaid.

By the mid-1970s AI researchers thought they had the answer – scripts and frames. A story about a restaurant, say, does not explain plates, knives, forks, kitchens, menus or waiters. It assumes the reader knows this information. But since a computer is ignorant of restaurants it must be given a restaurant script or frame[11], a kind of stereotypical scene containing knowledge of what events occur and in what order. Armed with this script or frame, so the researchers hoped, the computer

program could fill in the missing details of the story. But the script and frame writers were quickly defeated by the overwhelming complexity of general background knowledge.

The following simple passage shows what problems they encountered:

> Today was Jack's birthday. Penny and Janet went to the store. They were going to get presents. Janet decided to get a kite. 'Don't do that', said Penny. 'Jack has a kite. He will make you take it back.'

At first sight one might imagine that a birthday party frame with knowledge about cakes, parties, children, and presents might enable the computer not to get confused. But to understand even this simple story fragment, knowledge is required beyond anything one might put into a birthday party frame. The phrase 'Jack has a kite. He'll make you take it back' is especially problematic. As Dreyfus recalls 'in our culture children learn, if you get a new one just like the old one, you have to take the new one back,

155

not the old one. And the question was where are we going to store that information? It doesn't belong in the birthday party frame ... it doesn't belong in the department store frame, it's general background knowledge, the horrible thing, general background knowledge reared its head.'

The new Holy Grail for artificial intelligence research was common sense knowledge. What had started out as an exercise studying how people reasoned had turned into a quest for common-sense knowledge. The knowledge, as Minsky puts it, 'that every one shares. Everyone knows that if you hold something and release your grip it falls ... there's no person that you can communicate with who doesn't know the same things you do about space and time and social relations and geometry and language and whatnot. How large is this database that we all share, I suspect it's about ten million items or units, whatever units are.'

Minsky's figure comes from an assumption that a growing child learns something every ten seconds or so, but whatever the exact figure, it is undeniably very large.

How is it possible to acquire such a vast quantity of broad knowledge – the knowledge which every child has? Was this the end of AI?

Common-sense knowledge and how to get it

Doug Lenat was not about to give up. If general background knowledge was the key to human intelligence then how could a machine acquire the millions of things it needed to know? In Lenat's view:

> There are a couple of ways of getting that large knowledge base. One of them would be some elegant technique like build a natural language program and then have it read the material on-line to build up this big knowledge base. The problem with natural language understanding is that we have a kind of chicken and egg problem. It would be great to use as a way of building this knowledge base and yet we can't really do language understanding unless you already have common sense.

But, what about learning? In the late 1970s and early 1980s with programs like Eurisko, Lenat had tried getting computers to learn. While he had had limited success, he had realized that there was no real future in such programs because it was impossible to learn very quickly unless you already knew things to begin with. Learning has the property that we learn at the fringe of what we already know. So we learn that 'this thing is similar to something we know already, and here's the difference.' Thus the more one knows, the more and more quickly one can learn. The learning programs of computer scientists however started out with such little knowledge that they had a tiny fringe and didn't learn very well or quickly.

Lenat believed the only hope was to give the machine everything it needed to know so that it could understand natural language and learn. In 1984 he set up a project in Texas called CYC because it was likened to an encyclopedia project. The task, however, was not to make a computerized encyclopedia, but to input precisely the kind of common-sense knowledge that is 'not' found in encyclopedias, because it is 'too obvious to include'. Some of this knowledge is fundamental knowledge of space and time – ontological knowledge – so basic that nobody before has tried to codify it.

Take the entry in a typical encyclopedia on Abraham Lincoln. It tells the reader about his life and work but leaves out a vast amount of obvious information. The sentence: 'On January 2, Abraham Lincoln was in Washington.' implies but does not bother to mention that:

> Lincoln's left arm was probably in Washington as well, as were his feet, hair, skin and blood; His name was Abe Lincoln on January 1 and was on January 3 too.
>
> His parents were unaffected by where he was and remained his parents for life.
>
> For any interval of time within January 2, he was also in Washington.

The problems of explicitly codifying the world as it exists in the minds of human beings in order to represent it in a machine were so profoundly

157

difficult that many scientists, including some from the AI world, thought the CYC project a waste of time and money. Dreyfus, who by now had honed his arguments against the search for a disembodied artificial intelligence, felt it was bound to fail. It would fail, because the philosophers' dream of a disembodied rationality was false – a disembodied mind would always be brittle, it would always lack common sense. For a mind to have common sense, Dreyfus suspected, it needed a body.

" [Common-sense knowledge to a large extent] doesn't consist of facts... not a million facts... no number of facts. A lot of what we know is not factual knowledge at all, it's skills... Anybody who has children must be struck by the number of years they can spend playing around with blocks, playing around with sand, even just playing around with water just splashing it around, sopping it up, pouring it, splashing it. It seems endlessly fascinating to children. And one might wonder what are they doing? Why aren't they getting bored? How does this have any value? Well, I would say, they're acquiring the 50 000 water sloshing cases that they need for pouring and drinking and spilling and carrying water. And they've got their 50 000 cases of how solids bump in, scrape, stack on, fall off and common-sense knowledge would, in this story, I believe, consist in this huge number of special cases which aren't remembered as a bunch of cases, but which have tuned the neurons, so that, when something similar to one of these cases comes in, an appropriate action or expectation comes out. And that's what underlies common-sense knowledge. "

If intelligence depends on common sense and if Dreyfus was right that common sense has to be embodied in some way, then it followed that general-purpose human intelligence cannot be found in a blind, deaf and sensorially disabled machine.

The problem with this argument is that there are people who have little sensory contact with the world who nevertheless use language with common sense. In Oliver Sacks' collection of strange neurological tales, *The Man Who Mistook his Wife for a Hat*, he writes about a patient Madeleine J, born blind with cerebral palsy and unable to move her limbs. She never experienced her environment the way most children do by playing with blocks, pouring sand, swimming, drawing pictures, and riding a bicycle. She could not even read about it through braille. Practically everything she knew, the foundation on which she built her understanding of natural language, had been told or read to her. And Sacks reports she used language with common sense. Her skill at using language with common sense was not then based on experiencing what the words meant. It depended on her ability to process spoken language with an organ far more complex than any computer – her brain.

Even though she used her bodily senses very little, her intelligence was still embodied in a physical brain. Her brain learned by example and acquired skill at understanding stories by tuning its neurons. Perhaps there was no alternative to making intelligence the way nature did. Perhaps you first had to build a brain.

How to build a thinking machine 2. Build a brain

Leaving Doug Lenat with his CYC project in 1984, let us return to the early 1950s. From the beginning there were those who argued there was another and better way to make a thinking machine. Instead of trying to represent the world by programming a computer to be a mind, as Turing had suggested, why not build a brain, a physical machine which could learn from experiencing the world and which could construct its own model of it and base its own mind.

The human brain is made up of billions of neurons which are highly interconnected. There is no software in the brain. Experiences which come in through the senses trigger electrical signals to pass between the neurons. Patterns and regularities perceived by the senses are recorded and remembered as patterns of neural discharges.

While the brain is awesomely complex, from the early 1950s scientists like Frank Rosenblatt of Cornell University in New York State,

159

160

pursued the idea of building experimental, 'brain-like machines' called
perceptrons. Although primitive compared to the human brain, perceptrons
were similar in that they learned by
example rather than by being programmed. Perceptrons did especially
well at visual pattern recognition tasks
at which traditional AI had performed
poorly.

In 1960 at Cornell, Rosenblatt unveiled his Mark I perceptron
device. An array of 400 photocells,
which represented the neurons in the
retina, was wired to a set of association
units, each of which combined the electrical signals from several photocells
and relayed the signal to a bank of
response units. During training, the
Mark I 'looked' at a letter and guessed
what it was. After each guess its
human operator 'punished it' so to
speak if it failed by adjusting its connections appropriately. Then it tried
again.

In England, Dr Wilfred
Taylor of University College London,
trained his perceptron machine to
determine the subject's gender from
a photograph. In a special television
roundup of science and technology

called *Challenge 1963*, reporter
Raymond Baxter showed the machine
being trained on photographs, becoming temporarily confused by George
Harrison the Beatle (who had hair that
was untypically long for a man in
1963). The perceptron then identified
successfully the gender of new faces it
had never seen.

While promising, this
approach would virtually die out,
partly the result of the influence of
Marvin Minsky and Seymour Papert,
his co-director at the MIT Artificial
Intelligence Laboratory. Minsky and
Papert had studied perceptrons in the
early 1950s before abandoning them
for the digital computer. They felt that
while superficially appealing, perceptrons were not as promising a route
to 'Thinking Machines' as symbolic
artificial intelligence. In 1968 they
published an exhaustive work called
Perceptrons which many took as the
last word on the subject. This book
had a devastating effect on the field
and apart from a few solitary figures,
interest in building brain-like learning
machines disappeared until the end of
the 1970s.

By then 30 years of AI

had demonstrated very clearly its limits. Considerable advances in neurosciences had taught scientists much about how the brain handled vision and other processes. And most importantly, computers had increased dramatically in power, so that perceptron models could be more easily simulated to test their validity. The scene was set for a revival of the brain approach. This time the machines were called neural networks rather than perceptrons. A growing number of psychologists, physicists and neuro-scientists, began to argue that the original premise on which AI had been based was false. This movement became known as connectionism.

Architecture revisited

The artificial intelligentsia had claimed that the architecture of the hardware was unimportant to the mind on which it ran. But for tasks like vision it was clear that the classical von Neumann architecture was not up to the job (see box on p. 48). These tasks, which

required fast processing, needed parallel architecture of the sort found in brains and neural networks. In the words of Terry Sejnowski, a pioneer of the new wave:

> I don't want to know what a machine is capable of doing if it had all the time in the universe. There's a biological constraint. A machine should be able to do the computation in time that's comparable to human time. If that's your constraint, then the architecture of the machine makes all the difference in the world.[12]

But connectionists argued that in addition to architecture, there was a second more telling weakness of traditional AI – the programming problem. AI had sought to use software to simulate a mind and had had many successes. But the minds which played checkers and solved puzzles were smart small minds based on small programs. To build a mind with common-sense (putting billions of pieces of knowledge into a computer) involved perhaps trillions of lines of code – an unrealistic task. It could not be done without learning. Attempts

161

162

to get digital computers to learn had faltered. Neural nets, however, were learning machines. They were the way forward.

Terry Sejnowski has repeated the work of Wilfred Taylor, and developed a neural network that can distinguish male from female. he is certain that this time, the neural network approach will not die. His view is shared by many. Leon Cooper (the Nobel Prize-winning physicist) is building networks to do everything from recognizing handwriting to scrutinizing loan applications. Bernard Widrow developed a network which can steer an articulated truck as it reverses around a corner. At Carnegie-Mellon University in Pittsburgh, an automated road vehicle which had been controlled by a complicated rule-based AI system, is now running twice as fast under neural network control. The network, called NAVLAB, takes the input from a television camera and laser range-finder. The vehicle is driven by a human for a few minutes to train the net, which can then steer the vehicle automatically, unfazed by shadows and other vehicles.

But the small tasks neural networks can conquer are a far cry from the Holy Grail of common sense. NAVLAB has to be retrained if it rains. Sejnowski's gender recognizer cannot handle faces with beards and moustaches. They are micro-machines as limited as the microworlds of AI. And they have a problem which conventional software does not; researchers know little about how nets learn. This is important because what the net is learning may not be what the researchers think.

Early networks sprang some big surprises. One concerned a network that was trained to distinguish photographs of forests containing military tanks from photographs of forests without them. Scientists gave the network new pictures and it gave the right answers. But to double check, they snapped more photos and the network answered incorrectly each time. It emerged that the network was not distinguishing the presence or absence of tanks. By chance all the pictures with tanks had been taken on a sunny day, and all those without tanks on a cloudy day. What the net had learned to distinguish concerned how forests appear on cloudy and sunny days.

Classical AI had been stopped in its tracks by the common sense it needed to understand natural language. How likely is it that tiny neural networks will perform any better? As connectionists are the first to admit, progress will be slow. Only a few networks are concerned with language. One of the best known was aimed at teaching a network to associate patterns of letters with their sounds when read aloud, so to connect the word 'sight' with the sound 'site' for example. This network, devised by Terry Sejnowski and Charlie Rosen, was called NETalk.

Rules of pronunciation are fiendish. For example, 'the *e* is silent at the end of a word (sale, whale, male) except for pronouns like he, she, we, me'. NETalk did not try to figure out these rules. Instead, it was trained to carry out the task by association. 203 text input artificial neurons were connected to 80 so-called 'hidden units' which in turn were connected to each of the 26 output artificial neurons. Thus between the input and the output were 18 320 connections. Each of these connections had a

specific strength represented by a voltage. The higher the 'weight' as it is called, the stronger the connection and the greater its influence.

Each hidden unit takes all the information coming in, evaluates the strength and then decides on a weight of its own. This number is then passed on to every neuron in the output layer. The output layer combines the information and selects an output phoneme (speech sound). The network is connected to a speech synthesizer and sounds come out.

In the first training session NETalk was given a 1000-word text of a six-year-old's conversation, together with the sound of the child reading the text, transcribed by a linguist into the correct phonemes.

Initially, all the strengths of the connections were set at random and NETalk babbled like a child. This output was compared with what the output for the given text should be (the phonetic transcription of the child's speech), then the difference (the error) was sent back through the net or 'back propagated' as it is called. This adjusts the weights between the artificial neurons. The text was run

163

through NETalk again and again and each time the learning rule adjusted the connections between the neurons to make a better match. As it read the text over and over it began to pick up regular features. The synthetic sounds change from a babble to something vaguely understandable. The progress sounds not unlike a child learning to talk. After 16 hours of training the network could pronounce the text with 95 per cent accuracy. Even when it meets words it has never seen it can pronounce them fairly well.

It is easy to exaggerate the achievement of a neural network like NETalk. The net has learned simply to associate spelling patterns with patterns of pronunciation. It does not know what the words mean. In fact it understands much less about language than the ELIZA program.

Connectionists concede that they have just begun what might be a very long journey. How will connectionists get small networks like NETalk and NAVLAB to do more. So far, attempts to make neural networks bigger than a few hundred neurons backfire – the training time explodes. The brain with its 10

billion neurons has somehow managed to solve the problem. And the way it has solved it is instructive. The brain is not one machine but hundreds of smaller machines which have evolved to serve particular sense organs. Parts of the brain which deal with language and vision are sufficiently·distinct that stroke victims sometimes lose, as it were, part of their minds. One patient is unable to remember the names of things, another can't understand grammar, others can't recognize faces. In the normal brain these many machines for language, vision, movement etc. are combined in a highly complex act of integration. Somehow the brain has managed to co-ordinate lots of overlapping groups of neurons in pursuit of bigger goals. Probably this is how nature has evolved our general-purpose common sense and intelligence. Attempts to co-ordinate neural networks are in their infancy. It is not clear to many how to proceed.

Marvin Minsky is now convinced that any attempt to build an intelligent machine must reflect this underlying modularity of the brain. The key to a general intelligence is how the brain has co-ordinated this

164

society of machines to produce, as he calls it, the Society of Mind. In his view, research energies should be focused on finding ways to integrate smaller systems, be they symbolic AI programs or neural networks. This is where he encourages young researchers to go and work. But, he admits, it may be a very long term bet indeed.

So has AI failed? Not in the broad sense of the term. Within the next 10 years, thanks to AI research, robots guided by sonic waves will carry medicine trays between hospital nursing stations; semi-intelligent 'agents' will remind people of their appointments and select news clippings for them. Small amounts of Japanese will be translated simultaneously into English by a 'computerized' telephone.

AI, even in the strict sense, is still alive. One project – the CYC project – offers hope that the original dream of AI to create a general-purpose artificial intelligence can be achieved before the end of the century.

CYC – the last chance for symbolic AI

As we go to press some 3 million pieces of knowledge have been entered into CYC. Doug Lenat gives his project a success rate of between 60 and 70 per cent. Lincoln's left leg now travels with him in space, his birthday stays with him in time. CYC can interpret certain ambiguous phrases. It thinks 'a red conductor' could be a communist musician or red piece of conducting metal, but does not think it is a communist or an angry piece of conducting metal. It knows that 'Mary read Melville' means that Mary read one of Melville's books.

His team of knowledge codifiers, called CYCLISTS, are trying to capture the world to build a mind sufficiently knowledgeable to understand natural language and learn. Their work is fascinating. We watched them trying to capture the quintessential qualities of a nurse and feed the idea to CYC. CYC was told that nurses take temperatures, give medicine, are sympathetic and usually female. For better or worse, CYC

165

learns stereotypes.

Physically, CYC is more disabled than Oliver Sacks' patient, Madeleine J; CYC is all software, and no body. At night, while the rest of the team are asleep, CYC looks through its knowledge base identifying subtle inconsistencies[13], suggesting new generalizations and forming rudimentary analogies for Doug Lenat to sift through in the morning.

CYC says it has found a story about a man (Fred) with a razor confusing because as Lenat puts it:

> CYC's decided that Fred, while he's holding the razor in his hand, has some electrical parts, but on the other hand, it believes that in general, people don't have electrical parts. So it's trying to ask something here like, is Fred still a person while he's shaving. If so, how can he have electrical parts? So we'll have to explain that when you use something it doesn't actually become a part of you even though you can view the combined system as a single object if you want to.

Lenat apologizes for one of CYC's analogies:

> This is actually sort of rotten. It analogized that ownership is analogous to being married to someone. And also to being aware of something. That's actually very subtle. The idea that if you're aware of something, then in a way, you partially own that thing.

CYC goes on to argue that having a certain profession is analogous to being able to play a certain musical instrument. Lenat is unsure:

> I don't know. Do you think? I think that you could say that being a doctor or being a plumber is in some ways not that unlike being a flautist or a pianist. Namely there are certain instruments that you have talent and training to use. Boy, I'm already defending it, like a child here. That's pretty bad.

Will CYC succeed? It's too early to tell. Many scientists, including his colleagues in symbolic AI, think the problem is so hard that it is unlikely that Lenat will get it right. If his way of representing knowledge is flawed then CYC may not be able to learn very effectively, in which case, the project can only have limited success.

If CYC fails, we may be at the end of an era. But if it succeeds in passing the Turing Test for general natural language understanding, the payoff could be breathtaking. If CYC learns how to learn, its 'intelligence' in some areas might one day surpass our own. It is prospects like this that some people find alarming. Lenat takes a different view:

> " It is no more or less frightening in its own way than the thought, a hundred years ago or 150 years ago of some of the mechanical devices that would replace humans working on railroads. For example, the idea that there shouldn't be a machine that can travel faster than the horse, that there shouldn't be a machine that enables you to transmit messages faster than the Pony Express, that there shouldn't be machines that are better than hammering spikes into the ground than a human being with a hammer and so forth. Now today we look back and sort of smile at that and say, well that's not what's part of being human, that's not how I define myself... And similarly if you look at CYC as a kind of mental amplifier, as an intelligence amplifier, then I think you'll see that using it you'll be able to do things in a few decades that today people can't dream of doing. "

By the year 2000 we should know if general disembodied intelligence is possible. How it would be used (if it were possible) is uncertain. Lenat believes that in 20 years we will expect computers to have common sense in the same way that we expect them to be friendly today. CYC is, after all, just software and can be made available to all computers on disks, or more likely, as an on-line service.

Which brings us to the next and final chapter.

167

The digital age

As we have seen, most predictions about the social impact of computers have been wide of the mark. Initially, when computers were large and expensive, they were typically described as fearsome, semi-religious objects. They then became embroiled in the automation debate. Computers, it was argued, would take away people's jobs and produce enormous amounts of enforced leisure time. In a BBC documentary made in 1966, a spokesman for General Motors, predicted:

66 By the year 1990 or so we will first of all delay the entry of the working force into the labour market, [and] people will start to go to work at about age 25... We also think the retirement age will be coming down and that probably on average, retirement will occur at about age 50. And in the 25 years that will constitute the working part of a man's life, he will work about half what he works today, that is, he will have six months' vacation a year, or if he works an entire year at a 40-hour week, he will take next year off as a sabbatical year. I don't believe this is a pipe dream at all. I think this is merely a continuation of the trends that we've already seen in the last 50 years, and the impact the computer will have in mechanizing the white collar part of our economy. **"**

But people work at least as many hours today as they did in 1966 and have more or less the same amount of holiday each year. The computer has replaced some jobs, but has created many others. Equally, the notion of the computer as an Orwellian tool of the state has been overtaken by the advent of millions of small personal computers designed to empower individuals as much as the corporate establishment. Ironically, Orwellian societies of the Soviet block, which

had found it impossible to develop a sophisticated computer industry, found it equally impossible to prevent their people using microcomputers from the West to communicate and publish their ideas. In a wonderful twist of irony, John Sculley, the chief executive officer of Apple Computers, reports that President Gorbachev composed his thoughts about glasnost on a Macintosh.

But because many of the negative predictions about the computer have not materialized, does not mean we should be complacent, for the story of the computer is far from over. Perhaps the most challenging chapter is about to begin. In the next decade, we will see smaller, lighter computers, with elementary artificial intelligence applications like speech and character recognition. We will also witness a more fundamental development. For the world of the digital electronic computer is converging with that of another digital technology about which we have so far said little — electronic communications.

169

Marrying computers and telephones

On 11 September 1940, George Stibitz of Bell Labs staged a demonstration of an early relay computing machine (see Chapter 2) at Dartmouth University in New Hampshire. What made the demonstration remarkable was not simply his calculating machine but the fact that it was physically located hundreds of miles away in New York. Stibitz interacted with the device over a teletype line. Two decades later, Dartmouth University was again combining computers and telephones in its pioneering work on time sharing. This time the motive was simply economics. In the early 1960s remember, computers were costly; the marriage of computers and telephony enabled a scarce resource to be shared.

Until recently, however, the technology of the telephone was not digital but analog. It represented sounds by a continuous electrical signal that varied with alterations in air pressure. In contrast, a digital device digitizes sound by chopping up the electrical signals into many individual signals.

Telephone companies turned to digital electronics for many of the same reasons as the early computer makers. Digital integrated circuits are not only faster and more reliable than electromechanical relays, they bring enormous flexibility. Digital technology treats pictures, sounds, text, voices and computer data as bits, simple 0s and 1s. Once in this form, information can be communicated with less chance of error or degradation, but equally importantly, it can be processed and routed by software. A digital electronic telephone network is really a huge computer with all of the computer's strengths and weaknesses.

The world's information: a mouse click away

The convergence of computers and communications in a digital computer network marks a profound development in the history of communications. The computer allows users to manipulate and retrieve information from any text (and from all other media as well) in ways we can only just begin to imagine. In principle the knowledge of any subject or person in any work may be extracted at electronic speed. The entire Library of Congress – which some view as representing the accumulated knowledge of mankind – contains some 20 million books and pamphlets. In computer terms, however, the information stored in these texts is not so enormous. If it existed in electronic form the information would be held as some 18 trillion bits of information[1] and could be stored on 18 000 compact disks. It is not difficult to imagine a future in which material such as this is stored electronically, so that it can be accessed over a network. How long it would take to transfer the information depends on the speed of the network, which in turn depends on the band width of the information channel. With current technology, transmitting *the entire contents* of the Library of Congress over an ordinary telephone line would take some 1900 years. Over a modern fibre optic cable those 18 trillion bits would only take

23.5 hours. But the real advantage is that with sufficiently good search algorithms, data could be analyzed in ways a human librarian would find impossible. Scanning would take place at lightening speed with only relevant parts sent down the cable.

We have used the Library of Congress in this example because it is a central depository of books, pictures and films. But the thing about a computer network is that it is a distributed system. The network does not care where the information physically is. In principle, libraries of digitized works could be scattered all over the world, on different computers ranging from a desk top PC to a supercomputer. It would be possible to access the information from one computer in the network located in one city and then do the complex processing (the searching and extraction) on a different machine like a Connection Machine, which, because of its highly parallel architecture can do searches very quickly.

The media we invent help us to handle more complex tasks. The medium partly determines whether a task is feasible. Just as changing from

171

papyrus roles to vellum sheets enabled our predecessors to accomplish more complex tasks, storing the world's information in digital form is expected to have a similarly profound effect.

Electronic communities

There is another consequence of the merger of computers and communications which few predicted – the formation of new communities of people based not on geography but common interest.

As we have said, the original motive for combining computers with telephone networks was to distribute computers – a scarce and valuable resource. This was the idea behind time sharing. Similarly, the first dedicated computer network called ARPANET[2] was set up so scientists could share software and common databases. But soon people on the network also started using it to send messages to each other.

As Bob Lucky, an American pioneer of computer networking, recalls:

> ARPANET was originally built for computers to talk to computers and it was considered no place for a person out there. I mean you wouldn't want to be out there with all those bits flowing back and forth. But the computer operators started to send little messages back and forth between themselves that they would type in their terminal. And then those bits would be sent across the computer network and the computer operator at the other end would greet it as a message to him. And pretty soon, other people started using this new mechanism to send little pieces of electronic mail from person to person through the network.

ARPANET grew rapidly during the 1970s and 1980s and today, there are thousands of nodes in the network, servicing nearly 100 000 users worldwide. Now called INTERNET, it is a compelling demonstration of the power of computer networking. In linking scientists electronically, INTERNET has fostered a tremendous increase in international collaboration. And in some cases where scientific news has broken quickly, electronic mail has replaced scientific journals as the judge and jury of new discoveries and claims.

Enthusiasts of the new electronic frontier relate how they gather in an 'electronic town commons' or sit round 'a little electronic fire and trade wisdom'. But these gatherings are not geographic. Whereas the old town common was just for town people, many of whom grew up together, computer networking has raised the possibility of communities across the globe united by common interest.

Users are still developing social conventions but already so-called 'open' computer networks have some novel characteristics. Electronic communication among most of the groups is casual and democratic. It is acceptable to send electronic mail to company presidents, to people you might never dare telephone. Grammar, the correct layout and terms of address in letters and memos, are considered unimportant on most computer networks.[3]

The early users of computer networks like INTERNET spoke little about security and rules; they cherished the openness of the system. But this openness would be abused. In the late 1980s, a hacker from Germany accessed computers in Japan, Germany, Canada and the United States (including military computers) stealing information and clocking up huge telephone bills. The compelling story of how Cliff Stoll, a scientist at Lawrence Berkeley Laboratory in California, first discovered these abuses (through a 75 cent discrepancy in the Lab's computer bill) and then tracked the perpetrator through the world's computer networks is told in his book *The Cuckoo's Egg*[4] and is also the subject of a television documentary.

This was mild compared to the mayhem which broke out in November 1988 when a Cornell University graduate student, Robert Morris, released a 'worm' into INTERNET, crippling some 6000 military and university computers. A worm is a self-replicating program that infects terminals in a network, quickly propagating until the network collapses. Morris was suspended from Cornell and charged under the Com-

173

174

puter Fraud and Abuse Act. On 4 May 1990, he was sentenced to three years' probation, fined $10 000 and given 400 hours of community service.

New communities (real or virtual) evolve ways of protecting themselves. Electronic communities need security to exclude vandals and thieves. If a community is not physically isolated like a village, it has to restrict access in some other way via passwords, for example. Members of any community also need protection from particular interest groups within the community and they need privacy. Anthropologists have noted that privacy is more highly valued in complex societies. It follows that some of the openness and casu-

alness which the pioneers of electronic interchange found so pleasant will have to be sacrificed as electronic communities mature.

Glimpses of a networked future

Computer networking is in its infancy. In specialized communities like science and banking, networks have already changed work patterns. But how do computer networks affect the general public? In Britain and America, public use of computer networks is just beginning. In France and Singapore, however, computer networking has gone public

Computer 'hackers' cracking a network.

in a big way. Already we can see some of the benefits this new development offers, as well as some of the dangers.

France

In the late 1970s, the French telephone system was a shambles. Less than 10 per cent of the population had phones and more often than not, the phones did not work. In 1978, in a bold move, the government-owned telephone company, France Telecom, decided to upgrade dramatically their antiquated phone system and, at the same time, establish a national computer network that could be used by the general public. The idea was to provide a terminal to enable everybody to access on-line information. Minitel, as it was called, was launched on a commercial basis in 1983.

The first service offered on Minitel was a telephone directory. France Telecom gave away terminals free, in place of phone books. Customers were taught how to look up phone numbers on a on-line database. Giving away terminals cost France

Telecom millions of dollars, but it was part of a calculated plan to establish a large number of users.

From the beginning, just as with ARPANET, people quickly discovered that this information network could also be used for communication. By 1985, one of the most popular services was *messagerie*, a kind of cross between an electronic party-line and a personal ad column, which thousands of people used to share their erotic fantasies. The first messagerie service was set up by *Libération*, the third largest newspaper in France. *Libération* modelled its *messagerie* service, also called a 'chat line', on the personal ads it ran in the back of its daily paper. It was a terrific success: in 1987 *Libération* earned more than 2 million dollars from their chat lines.

Today Minitel offers more than 15 000 services covering everything from finance and travel to pet shows. Roughly two out of every five people in France use at least one Minitel service. After 10 years of investment by France Telecom, Minitel is expected to turn a profit next year – the only videotex, or public information system, in the

175

world to do so. One big reason may be cost. With Minitel, unlike the phone system, there is no such thing as long distance. The cost for a service is the same whether it is across the street, or across the country.

In 1986, France was embroiled in a wave of student strikes. Students around the country protested in the streets against government plans to restrict admission to government-subsidized universities. But what ministers did not realize was that the students had a new weapon — Minitel. The students used the Minitel network because the 'movement' was spread all over France and they wanted a quick way to communicate between organizers and universities, and to gather information on the mood of the public.

With the help of *Libération*, David Assouline and other leaders of the movement established two different services. First, a public service where people could read the latest events or express their support or outrage. And second, a private service with secret passwords which the protesters used to organize their activities. On 27 November, more

than one million people marched through the streets of Paris while the leaders of the movement met with key government ministers. It had been an effective campaign. The students' success using Minitel was not missed by other political groups. As Assouline says: 'We were the first to use Minitel in the way we did ... Now it is used widely by TV and radio for opinion polls.'

But computer networks have a sinister side too. For an intelligent network *knows* about the people and computers which use it. It must know to connect the user with the person he wants to communicate with or the information he needs. Every event which happens in a network leaves an electronic trace. Unless specifically instructed otherwise, networks monitor themselves. In the wrong hands the information they automatically gather can be dangerous.

This danger can be best seen in a society which has embraced computer networking probably more completely than any other — Singapore.

Singapore – the return of Big Brother?

It is something of an irony that the most pervasive and futuristic use of networking is not in New York, or in any European city. It is not even in Japan. If you want to have a look at a networked future you will find it in Singapore, a small island nation in Southeast Asia.

In the words of the minister of trade and industry, Brigadier General Lee, son of Lee Kuan Yew, until a year ago the prime minister of Singapore, the country had no alternative:

" [Singapore is] a small country of 2.5 million people who depend on [their] wits for a living. We have no natural resources. We have no hinterland, no continental catchment to bring people in – the best and the brightest – as Washington, New York or Boston would have. We've just got Singaporeans and we make a living by plugging into the world, keeping up to date, trading, manufacturing, investing, banking, communicating, making ourselves relevant to a global economy. "

In short, Singapore's leadership has decided the island's future lies in being an information economy based on computer networks; a small nation which can shuffle information around better than anyone else. In just a few years, computer networks have infiltrated almost all aspects of Singapore society from the government and industry to the home. The motive is the relentless pursuit of efficiency.

One example of Singapore's prowess in information systems is Tradenet, a computer network that links all the shippers and air cargo companies with the customs office. Packages coming into or out of Singapore must pass review by several government agencies. In the past, this meant days of delay as documents wound their way through the bureaucracy. With the Tradenet network, clearing customs takes a couple of minutes.

177

Tradenet, like most networks, consists of desk-top computers connected by phone lines to a central machine. This central computer, acting like a huge and exceptionally fast telephone switchboard, directs the trader's electronic document to all the necessary government agencies simultaneously. Within minutes the trader receives a response through the network. Set up on an experimental basis in 1987, Tradenet is now used by almost all Singapore's shippers.

One of the island's latest computer networks is Medinet, which connects hospitals with the government-run insurance programme. The system tracks individual patients and submits insurance claims forms automatically. Since data is transmitted along the network at electronic speeds, distance is no obstacle. Patients can be in one location, the central computer in another, and consulting physicians on the other side of the island. Doctors can also use the system to tap into databases in the United States such as the cancer database operated by the National Cancer Institute.

Computer networks are reaching into the home as well. With a new national information system called Teleview, people can shop and bank from home. This videotex system also carries educational programmes and news bulletins. When the system is fully implemented in three years, the whole of Singapore society will be wired up. So far, people seem to have embraced computer networking, agreeing with the government's vision of an information-based future. But there is a dark side. The island's economy in particular, and the society in general, are closely managed by a government preoccupied with efficiency. The same networks which enable efficiency allow monitoring. Armed with the rationale of achieving ever increasing efficiency in social planning, the government are using those networks to monitor many aspects of daily life.

Singapore is a compact island 26 miles long and 14 miles wide and it is possible to digitize most aspects of its infrastructure. The Land Data Hub is a network which stores data from maps in electronic form.

This system gives planners the information they need about any particular building – which phone lines it uses, which businesses are inside and who owns them. In Singapore it would be impossible for the Gas Board to dig up the road one week and the Electricity Company the next, without either one being aware of the other. Land Hub is an electronic vision of Singapore itself. It makes planning more efficient, but when the database is complete, the government will know how every square foot of the country is used – who is using it, and for what.

Other networks being developed by the government keep records of where people live and work. The Establishment Data Hub, for example, contains a wealth of information about businesses in Singapore including material on their employees. The People Data Hub, now being developed, will contain detailed information on every Singapore citizen. With all these databases, linked by networks, few activities will be free from government attention. For Brigadier General Lee this does not present a moral dilemma:

> ❝ We do quite a number of things which Western governments probably would hesitate to do, either because ideologically they feel that they should not intrude on personal lives or sometimes because they just don't have the time to do it because the next election is too close around the corner. But it is a different society and we have to govern the way the population needs to be governed and the way the population accepts being governed. ❞

179

The problem in Western societies like Britain and America is not government monitoring but monitoring by commercial interests and networks. Minimal restrictions exist on what people can use computer networks for and abuses are common. Typical is the case of TWA ticketing agents who work on keyboards while answering phone calls. This gruelling work is made even worse because the company monitors the productivity of workers by recording their number of key strokes, the time they spend on the phone, when they leave their desks

180

for lunch or to go to the toilet. Such practices, an electronic version of those used in Dickensian sweatshops are widespread. Other problems flow from the interconnectedness of databases. The great advantage of not having to re-enter information and of accessing information in other databases has to be measured against the problem of erroneous information spreading throughout the networks. When mistakes occur they can prove difficult to correct. One story was cited in the *Los Angeles Times* of a man, Forman Brown, who a network (by mistake) thought was dead. His checks started coming back to him with the words 'deceased' stamped on them. His problem spread to the Social Security Office which didn't want to pay his State Pension and to Medicare, who refused to reimburse him for doctors' bills incurred after he had officially died.

To err is human

66 An undetected error in a logarithmic table is like a sunken rock at sea yet undiscovered. 99

John Herschel, 1842.[5]

66 The electronic switches that run the telecommunications network today, have 2 million lines of code. It's guaranteed that they're not all right, that there have to be mistakes in it. They're just waiting to happen. 99

Bob Lucky, head of research at AT&T Bell Labs, 1990.

The attractions of digital electronics are many. A person dialling a toll free call anywhere in the United States will have their call routed automatically to the right office. Software will chose the best route, software will decide whether the message flows through copper wires, glass fibres, or is bounced off a satellite. The flexibility of a digital network is remarkable, and is what enables telephone companies from British Telecom to AT&T to provide services like forwarding calls, conference calls and itemized billing. But with a digital computerized system comes a kind of complexity which we, as yet, only dimly understand how to manage.

In Chapter 6 we touched on the problems of writing complex software and the difficulties of tracing bugs. Without wishing to create alarm, we will return to this subject and add a twist. It is one thing to have a software bug in a stand-alone computer and quite another in a network where many people are dependent on the proper workings of the electronic community.

Bad software can be a life or death matter.[6] Consider the astonishing case of the Therac 25, a radio-therapy machine used to treat cancer patients by giving carefully tailored doses of radiation to destroy tumours. In 1985 and 1986 faulty software led to the deaths of four people.

One patient who survived, Katy Yarborough, was supposed to get 200 units of radiation, but because of a software error she received 20 000. She was burned and paralyzed on her left side, but the hospital denied any fault. As the Therac 25 had been used thousands of times before, they argued, they could not be held responsible. A similar incident happened with a Therac in Texas. Ray Cox, a 33-year-old, receiving treatment for a tumour on his back felt a sharp bolt of heat. Technicians inspected the machine and, not finding anything wrong, put it back in service.

But when another patient Vernon Kidd screamed with pain during his treatment, it was investigated again, and this time a fault was found; not in the hardware but in the software. Cox and Kidd later died.

Faulty software can cost millions. On 20 November 1985, a computer in the Bank of New York, poised to process 32 000 government securities transactions, started to overwrite the records. With the records gone the bank did not know who to bill for which securities. But since the New York Federal Reserve continued to charge them for the securities, the bank ended the day $32 billion overdrawn. The bank borrowed to cover the deficit, and although they eventually sorted out the mess, the interest on the bridging loan cost $5 million.

The stories get worse. At London's Heathrow Airport on Saturday, 6 August 1988, the heavily computerized air-traffic control system failed. Breakdowns are not uncommon. The software used at Heathrow – the National Airspace Package – consists of about 1 million lines of code that took about 2000 man years to

181

write and develop. It was converted from American software. Adapting software often produces errors, yet we depend on the Heathrow system to keep our planes from crashing. Humans are still involved in traffic control but without the computer they are powerless. And they must believe what the software tells them. The aircraft they track are themselves loaded with software which controls everything from the navigation system to the cabin temperature.

There is an extraordinary irony about where the history of computers may be leading us. Remember that Babbage's motivation to build his Difference Engine was the inability of human beings to produce error-free tables. These tables were the reference works on which scientists and engineers in the nineteenth century depended, and mistakes in tables could translate into errors in the real world, like ships going aground. Now we have the electronic descendants of Babbage's Difference and Analytical Engines which have conquered arithmetic and generally make few mistakes. Today the task with which humans struggle is writing software.

The parallels with the past are uncanny. As with the volumes of tables in the nineteenth century, huge software programs involving millions of instructions are often not written from scratch. Instead existing software is modified. Like a faulty figure in a table which is entered into a complex calculation, a mistake in a line of computer code can have serious consequences.

Can humans write software programs with millions of lines of code without errors? Until January 1989, many people held up the software used to control the 114 computers in the AT&T long-distance telephone network as proof of highly complex yet flawless software.[7] But at 2:25 p.m. on Monday, 15 January 1989 (luckily a holiday), the system failed. Users received busy signals when they tried to call long distance. About half of the national and international calls did not connect. Businesses highly dependent on the telephone descended into chaos. American Airlines claims to have lost about two-thirds of its estimated 300 000 daily calls. Car rental firms, hotels, telemarketing firms were all badly hit. Part of the network still functioned – a part based on older technology. By 11:30 that night engineers had resolved the problem which lay in the supposedly infallible software.

The malfunction occurred in a switch which routed telephone calls from the New York metropolitan area. A small mistake in one of the millions of lines of computer code that governs the network caused one switch to send out alarm messages to other switches in the network, which prevented them from sending calls to the correct destinations. The error had originated during a software upgrade – to improve the service to customers by cutting down the time they would have to wait between dialling and ringing. Bob Lucky explains:

> Computer networks are very robust in one sense and fragile, vulnerable in another sense. You could go out and physically damage networks, drop bombs on them, cut lines and they'd still work. You could drop bombs all over this country and make a call between New York and Los Angeles. And yet they're vulnerable to little information damages. They're vulnerable to viruses or mistakes in computer programs that run them. The electronic switches that run the telecommunications network today have 2 million lines of code. It's guaranteed that they're not all right, that there have to be mistakes in it. It's beyond human possibility to make it entirely right.

Digital computers and computer networks are examples of discrete state machines. They have billions of different logical states. An error in just one step can produce an effect not only impossible to predict but difficult to debug – in the AT&T case one mistake affected the whole system. As engineers say, digital systems do not degrade gracefully.

Human beings are mediocre at programming. Programmers, even good ones, typically make a handful of mistakes every 1000 lines of code. Even with scrupulous checking in a huge project with a million lines of code, it is virtually impossible to eliminate error. Errors simply must remain. Babbage's lifelong friend, John Herschel, writing in

183

184

support of Babbage's efforts to mechanize calculation warned: 'An undetected error in a logarithmic table is like a sunken rock at sea yet undiscovered.' A long program may appear perfect, but inside may be a bug which is harmless until a particular set of circumstances occurs. An error is like a time bomb, or, to use Herschel's metaphor, a concealed rock. But the consequences when everything is networked from banks to hospitals may be much worse than a ship going aground.

The problem of managing software complexity has sparked intense debate. Appeals have been made for software to be subjected to rigorous engineering standards. Programs, it is argued, should be *engineered* like roads and bridges. Appeals have been made for computer programs to be verified mathematically. It has even been suggested that programmers should be certified like accountants (which became mandatory after the 1929 stock market crash). But none of these suggestions seems feasible. Computer programs capable of mathematically verifying large programs are as long as the programs themselves. To test software empirically by running every conceivable branch, option or permutation would, in many cases, take hundreds of years. The most that can be done is to subject parts of these programs – the parts computer scientists think are critical – to empirical or mathematical verification.

Doubtless, humans will find a way to cope with this complexity. The trend in programming languages towards so-called object-oriented programming (an innovation developed but not invented at Xerox PARC), which packages software into 'objects' which are the close analogues of what they represent in the real world, looks promising. A typical software unit might be a software beam, which looks and behaves like a beam on the screen and contains all the knowledge of the physics of beams. By thinking of the problem in an analogue way, and using their natural intuitions, programmers, it is hoped, will be less likely to commit errors.

An unfinished story

As we enter the last decade of the twentieth century with computer scientists grappling with the problems and opportunities of networked computing, it is as well to remember that it is early days yet.

The history of the computer began as a quest for a machine to free mankind from drudgery and error, a quest which led to the concept of a general-purpose machine. Remarkably, it had turned out that any machine general enough to handle all arithmetic could, in principle, also be programmed to perform any mental process which could be stated in a clear, step by step manner.

For speed, computer designers during the Second World War had been compelled to choose electronic technology to build their machines, and entered a digital electronic realm where the usual constraints of scale and size did not apply. Mechanical (or even electro-mechanical) computers might not have changed the world greatly, as scaling them up would surely have

proved impossible. Assuming that Babbage's Analytical Engine could have been built, how would one have been constructed 10 times, a hundred times or a million times faster?

In the electronic digital realm, however, increasingly powerful computers could be built which were smaller and more reliable. Potential barriers to advance such as the tyranny of numbers were overcome and innovations such as the integrated circuit and microchip led to a curve of improvement, unparalleled in engineering history. Whereas today's fastest aircraft only fly tens of times faster than the first planes, today's computers are millions of times more powerful than the ENIAC. The spectacular and continuing improvements in computer hardware are now taken for granted, so much so that the insides of computers have lost their interest for all but the specialist engineer. There are no visible moving parts, just ever smaller and more versatile chips. While one day we will run up against the limits of miniaturization dictated by the laws of physics, at the moment quite some mileage remains. Much of what has happened in recent computer

185

186

history rests on this stunning engineering achievement. Processing power could be 'wasted' on making computers easy to use, which in turn enabled people other than computer scientists to discover them and dream up uses for them.

As we have seen, early visionaries like Turing glimpsed the computer's general-purpose nature and the implications of this for artificial intelligence. They did not imagine that it would be ubiquitous. And they never understood that it was really a new medium rather than a machine, one that would (like previous media), begin rooting itself in our culture and affecting our attitudes and thoughts.

The marks, which in Babylonian times were used to record information, led to a system of writing which enabled highly sophisticated societies to evolve. The same marks enabled wonderful patterns of thought and human interaction from poetry to opera to be transmitted through generations. The rapidly switching electronic pulses inside the ENIAC, which meant wartime computers could do ballistics calculations at superhuman speed, led to a machine that has permeated our world. Few people would doubt that the complex forms of social organization and interaction which today we take for granted are made possible by the digital electronic computer. And just as the terse messages on cuneiform tablets evolved (from recording bushels of wheat, for example) to recording great literature, so too these early mundane uses of the computer will evolve into something much grander than banking and air travel.

We have argued that the computer is not so much a machine as a powerful personal medium of expression and communication. If current trends continue, computers will soon be portable and inexpensive like books. They will be networked together so they can access written knowledge in new ways. But the computer is not confined to text, and can conjure up and manipulate different media from images to musical sounds. With modern computers, we can, for the first time, immerse ourselves in a sophisticated three-dimensional illusion; we can experience the products of our own imaginations —

walk through an unbuilt building or construct a previously unsynthesized molecule.

That computers make these activities possible is certain. What is less certain is whether people will use computers in the ways suggested, or whether they will, as in the past, discover other outlets. Of all the technologies we have invented, the computer has been the most difficult to interpret and predict. Forty years ago scientists sincerely believed that the world would need only a handful of computers. Will the uses to which we are putting computers seem similarly naïve 40 years from now? It will be up to Lara Pullan and her generation to decide where we take computers from here.

In its short history the computer has left few areas of life untouched. Our narrative has involved not only science, engineering, and business, but delved into human perception, intelligence and communication. So far, the computer has empowered the human mind and illuminated our understanding of it, rather than replaced it. Despite the colossal changes the computer has wrought, despite the superhuman things the computer can do, it is still a machine dependent on the human beings who write its software, who are as fallible as the human computers of Babbage's day. Unless we accept this truth and build it into our plans, we may face some extraordinary setbacks as we explore the digital electronic networked frontier to which the computer has led us.

187

Footnotes

Introduction

1 See Turing's famous paper, 'On Computable Numbers, with an Application to the Entscheidungsproblem', Proceedings of the London Mathematical Society, 2nd series, volume 42, part 3, November 12, 1936, 230–265.

2 Simon Lavington, *Early British Computers* (Bedford, Mass.: Digital Press 1980) p. 104.

3 J. Presper Eckert (see page 37) said of Dr Howard Aiken: Dr Aiken had a different concept of the use of computers than Mauchly and I did. According to his concept, six machines of the capability of the UNIVAC would have done the entire needs of the United States. Since a modern microprocessor is faster than six UNIVACs, this means that a modern microprocessor would be sufficient for all the computer needs of the United States. Now he quickly realized this was wrong.

Chapter one

1 Charles Babbage, *Passages From the Life of a Philosopher*, 1864, Reprinted in *The Works of Charles Babbage*, Martin Campbell-Kelly (Ed.), (Pickering, Vol. XI, 1989).

2 H.W. Buxton, *Memoirs of the Life and Labors of the Late Charles Babbage Esquire, FRS.* (Charles Babbage Institute Reprint Series for the History of Computing, vol. XIII, 1988) p. 46.

3 Babbage was not the first to suggest a printing calculator. This distinction belongs to Johann Helfrich Müller, a German engineer, who suggested such a device although he did not design or build one. Müller is also credited with the first known documented suggestion, in that same year, of using the method of differences as the basis for mechanization. This method reduces complex calculations involving multiplication and division to simple additions. It is almost certain that Babbage was ignorant of these events and conceived of his designs independently.

4 The collapse of what was probably the first government-funded research and development project in computing is a fascinating case study of issues that find strong echoes today. Babbage regarded the cultural climate for entrepreneurial ventures as unfavourable. He held uncannily familiar views on the now common allegation that Britain can innovate but is unable to exploit her inventiveness. In 1852 he wrote: Propose to an Englishman any principle, or any instrument, however admirable, and you will observe that the whole effort of the English mind is directed to finding a difficulty, a defect, or an impossibility in it. If you speak to him of a machine for peeling a potato, he will pronounce it impossible; if you peel a potato with it before his eyes, he will declare it useless, because it will not slice a pineapple. Impart the same principle or show the same machine to an American, or to one of our colonists, and you will observe that the whole .effort of his mind is to find some new application of the principle, some new use for the instrument.' 'Thoughts on the Principle of Taxation with Reference to a Property Tax and Its Exceptions' (1852). In *The Works of Charles Babbage*, Martin Campbell-Kelly (Ed.), vol. V, 1989, p. 41.

5 A full size Difference Engine No. 2 has been built at the Science Museum in London to commemorate the 200th anniversary of Babbage's birth in 1791. The engine is built to original designs from materials that closely match those that would have been available to Babbage.

6 Article 1, Section 2 of the US Constitution mandates the Census Bureau to complete the census within a decade.

Chapter two

1 *Pioneers of Computing*, Recorded Interview No. 2, London Science Museum, 1975.

2 Zuse did learn of Charles Babbage in 1939 when he tried to obtain a patent for one of his first mechanical models.

3 Notable among such analogue machines was Vanevar Bush's gigantic Differential Analyzer which he developed to help solve differential equations (involving continuous functions) pertinent to electrical power networks.

4 Paul Ceruzzi, an American computer historian along with others, argues that Zuse never totally agreed with Schreyer that vacuum tubes were better and that after the Second World War, Zuse continued building electromechanical relay calculators, some of which were commercially successful

189

and, like the Z11, were still in use in the 1980s. An interview with Zuse in the mid-1970s indicates less than total enthusiasm for vacuum tubes.

5 *Pioneers of Computing*, Recorded Interview No. 16, London Science Museum, 1980.

6 The idea of making an electronic calculator to help solve sets of linear equations occurred to a physics professor at Iowa State College at Ames called John V. Atanasoff in 1937. By the end of 1939, Atanasoff and his graduate assistant, Cliff Berry, had built a prototype machine which could add and subtract binary numbers. The ABC, which they built subsequently, was a kind of electronic Difference Engine in that it was hard-wired to solve only one kind of problem – systems of linear equations. It worked intermittently up until 1942 when the project was dropped. In December 1940, John Mauchly met John Atanasoff and subsequently visited him in Iowa and saw his partially completed ABC machine. Many years later this visit featured in a court case.

Sperry Rand's patent on the computer (which had been granted for the ENIAC to Mauchly and other members of the team and acquired during the merger of Sperry with Remington Rand) was being challenged by Honeywell. The challenge was based on the assertion that the patent was invalid because Mauchly's idea for the ENIAC derived from Atanasoff's work and influence. In 1973, Judge Larson of the US District Court in Minnesota, agreed ruling the patent invalid. His ruling is seen as a victory for the Atanasoff camp, who passionately push his cause. See Clark R. Mollenoff, *Atanasoff: Forgotten Father of the Computer* (Iowa State University Press, 1988). But most historians do not take the ruling seriously and believe that, whatever Atanasoff's achievement, it does not compare to or diminish what Eckert and Mauchly achieved in building the ENIAC.

Others, in addition to Zuse, sought to build electromechanical relay calculating machines; notably, George Stibitz of Bell Telephone Laboratories between 1939 and 1946, and Howard Aiken of Harvard University who unveiled his Mark 1 in August 1944. For a discussion see Paul Ceruzzi, *Reckoners*, (Greenwood, 1983) and his chapter 'Relay Calculators' in W. Aspray (Ed.), *Computing before Computers*, (Iowa State University Press, 1990).

7 Resurrection: Bulletin of the Computer Conservation Society, Autumn, 1990, p. 4.

8 B.E. Carpenter and R.W. Doran (Eds.), *A.M. Turing's ACE Report of 1946 and Other Papers* (MIT Press, 1986). A full discussion is in Andrew Hodges' excellent book *Alan Turing: The Enigma* (Simon & Schuster, 1983).

9 Lecture to London Mathematical Society, 20 February 1947, quoted from Hodges, ibid, pp. 318–320.

Chapter three

1 See R.F. Clippinger's discussion in 'Mathematical Requirements for the Personnel of a Computing Laboratory', *American Mathematical Monthly*, 57 (1950) p. 439.

2 These four customers ordered six computers between them.

3 IBM *had* funded scientific computers. They had supported Howard Aiken in the Second World War and built the SSEC (Selective Sequence Electronic Calculator) – a hybrid relay and vacuum tube machine. But these were special scientific machines built to support the war effort and education.

4 The Bank of America estimated that it would need 30 ERMA machines and invited manufacturers to bid on the job. By this time, there were six big computer companies in the United States. Dominated by IBM, they would come to be known as IBM and the BUNCH – Burroughs, UNIVAC, NCR, Control Data, General Electric (GE), RCA and Honeywell. Half of these companies bid on the ERMA project but none of them got the contract. It went instead to General Electric. The Bank of America did not know that GE had never made a computer and was not in the computer business.

Like IBM, GE had had internal arguments about the wisdom of entering the computer business, and in 1959 the president, Ralph Cordiner, had decided against it. He held that GE was not a business machine company and should not make such a complex machine. But one employee, Barney Oldfield, thought differently and refused to take no for an answer. On hearing about the Bank of America project, he took some plain GE stationery and had the words 'computer division' printed in the corner. Without the knowledge or backing of GE management, he sent a proposal to Bank of America.

Oldfield, who knew little about the economics of computers, had proposed building the ERMA system for $30 million – half of what the other companies had offered. The Bank of America, ever mindful of the bottom line and unaware that GE had never produced a computer, accepted the bid. Remarkable as it seems, construction started on the computer inside the GE building itself without Cordiner knowing. When the first ERMA computer was ready to be demonstrated, Barney Oldfield invited a host of GE managers, including Cordiner, to view their new creation.

Cordiner was shocked and angry. He fired Oldfield on the spot and gave orders for GE to remove itself from the computer business immediately. Oldfield has not been heard of since. But GE did not leave the computer business – at least not for a while.

Chapter four

1 Quoted in Michael F. Wolff, 'The Genesis of the Integrated Circuit', *IEEE Spectrum*, August 1976, p. 45.

2 Originally Texas Instruments used the term 'solid state microelectronics', while Fairchild called their devices 'micrologic'. The term 'integrated circuit' was first used by Motorola and stuck. See *Electronics*, 5 January, p. 63.

3 Lincoln Labs was a large research centre set up by MIT to supervise the development of SAGE (Semi-Automatic Ground Environment), an air defence system. MIT had been commissioned by the Defense Department because it operated the world's only real-time computer in 1950 – the Whirlwind. In the early 1950s, Jay Forrester and his team pioneered many concepts which were vital to the development of interactive computing. These included computer monitors, which not only displayed the aircraft being tracked, but also enabled the operators to communicate with the computer through aspects of the display itself. Forrester's team also pioneered the use of magnetic core memory – little doughnuts of iron strung on a grid of wires, which could, depending on the direction of magnetization, store a '1' or a '0'. One of the principal designers of Whirlwind, Wes Clark, went on to design what is generally regarded as the first desk-size 'personal' computer in the early 1960s called LINC. It was an experimental machine, and its importance lay in how it influenced a generation of young computer scientists to think about the possibility of smaller, more personal, computers.

4 Douglas C. Engelbart, 'A Conceptual Framework for the Augmentation of Man's Intellect' in *Vistas in Information Handling*, vol. I, Paul William Howerton and David C. Weeks, (Eds.), (Washington: Spartan Books, 1963), p. 14.

5 SDS was a computer company that established a niche in the market by focusing on science and engineering, areas in which IBM had little interest. But they were not a forward-looking company and had rejected Taylor's efforts (when he was at ARPA) to persuade them to convert their batch processing machines to time sharing. At the time of their sale to Xerox the company was sinking fast. Indeed Max Palevsky, the one-time chairman of SDS, reported after selling the company for $900 million, 'We sold them a dead horse before it hit the ground.' The PARC scientists refused to use the SDS machines and preferred to build their own from scratch. For a thorough discussion of the Xerox PARC affair see Douglas K. Smith and Robert C. Alexander, *Fumbling the Future: How Xerox Invented, then Ignored, the First Personal Computer*, (William Morrow, 1988).

6 To find a medium as versatile as pen and paper, Thacker was led to consider raster displays. Television uses a raster display in which the screen image is made up of adjacent parallel lines scanned in quick succession onto the screen by an electron beam. Thacker saw that a computer could manipulate a screen image if it was treated as being made up of a very fine grid of independent elements. The status of each tiny element (brightness, later colour) could be stored as a word in the computer's memory and the picture could be manipulated in memory element by element. Because of the one-to-one correspondence between bits in the computer's memory and the elements on the screen, the image produced in this way is called 'bit mapped'.

Chapter five

1 In August 1990, the semiconductor world was rocked when it was announced that Gilbert Hyatt, a 52-year-old inventor had been granted a patent on the microprocessor. Gilbert Hyatt, claims to have discovered the microprocessor before Hoff in 1968. He filed his patent in 1970. It is too early to predict the consequences.

Chapter six

1 Jobs was forced to leave the company shortly afterwards in a classic power

193

struggle with John Sculley, the chief executive officer, whom Jobs had lured to Apple from Pepsi Cola. The sordid tale is chronicled in Frank Rose's *West of Eden* (Penguin, 1989). For a different angle read John Sculley's *Odyssey: Pepsi to Apple . . . a Journey of Adventure, Ideas and the Future*, (Harper & Row, 1987).

2 A number of historians of writing have suggested that numeracy predates literacy. For example Roy Harris in his book *The Origin of Writing*, (Open Court, 1986) argues:

Almost certainly *homo sapiens* mastered the use of numbers before mastering the use of letters. What is being suggested here is something else: that the human race had to become numerate in order to become literate. No society which could not count beyond three ever achieved writing; at least not by its own efforts.

Counting is associated in many cultures with primitive forms of recording information which have a graphically isomorphic basis, i.e., there is a one-to-one correspondence between the number of items and the number of marks scratched on a tablet. In this argument the abstraction and representation of a 'number' leads to the abstraction and representation of other things in writing. If this is true it shows a wonderful consistency with what has happened in the history of computers.

3 Alan Kay has been talking and writing about the computer being a medium for over 20 years. In the late 1960s he had a vision of what he called a 'dynabook' (a dynamic book) – a portable book-sized computer which could do anything with information. Computers seem to be heading this way, although currently, portables are expensive and limited in their powers.

4 Brooks is himself something of a software philosopher. See his book *The Mythical Man Month*, (Addison-Wesley, 1982).

Chapter seven

1 Edward A. Feigenbaum, 'What Hath Simon Wrath?' (unpublished).

2 Logic Theorist proved 38 of the first 52 theorems in Chapter 2 of the *Principia*. While Russell was amused to hear that one of the proofs was more elegant than his own, the *Journal of Symbolic Logic* allegedly refused to publish an article co-authored by Logic Theorist on the grounds that it was not a human being.

3 It is said that IBM (who were trying to promote the image of the computer

as a dumb data processor) were embarrassed by the activities of Samuels and Bernstein and tried to keep them out of the media. To make matters worse, one of the four organizers of the conference was another IBM person, Nathaniel Rochester. The others were Claude Shannon, John McCarthy and Marvin Minsky.

4 Claude Shannon had published an article in 1950 in *Scientific American* called 'A Chess-Playing Machine', which no doubt influenced many of the conferees.

5 Quoted in M. Mitchell Waldrop, *Man-Made Minds: The Promise of Artificial Intelligence* (Walker, 1987), p. 34.

6 Much of this work formed the basis for the kind of factory robots that pick and inspect items. They are now commonplace.

7 Man asserted his supremacy over machine by ridiculing the efforts of these early translators. One joke circulating at the time related to a computer that could reputedly translate English into Russian and vice versa. At the inaugural demonstration, the computer was given the English adage, 'Out of sight, out of mind' to translate into Russian and back into English. It finally printed on its output terminal: 'The invisible are insane.'

8 Today, by restricting the size of the vocabulary, researchers are having more success. Matsushita in collaboration with Carnegie-Mellon University is in the process of bringing out a 'translating telephone' which translates Japanese into English (and other languages) simultaneously.

9 J. Lighthill. *A Report on Artificial Intelligence*, Science Research Council, 1972, p. 17.

10 The second edition of this book was retitled *What Computers Can't Do: The Limits of Artificial Intelligence* (Harper & Row, 1979). More recently he has written, together with his brother Stuart Dreyfus, *Mind Over Machine: The Power of Human Intuition and Expertise in the Era of the Computer*, (The Free Press, 1986). Also see his and other contributions in 'Artificial Intelligence', *Daedelus*, vol. 117, No. 1, Winter 1988.

11 Roger Shanks pioneered the use of scripts, drawing a metaphor from a screenplay. Marvin Minsky and his colleagues represented knowledge in frames.

12 Quoted in W. Allman *Apprentices of Wonder*, (Bantam, 1989), p. 177.

13 CYC's knowledge is organized in categories. As for us, knowledge must be consistent within a category, but

195

knowledge from different categories can be contradictory. For example, the two sentences '*Dracula was a vampire*' and '*Vampires don't exist*' are not actually contradictory. The first belongs to a fictional category the second, to a factual category of what does and does not exist in the real world.

Chapter eight

1 Figures quoted from Robert W. Lucky, *Silicon Dreams: Information, Man and Machine*, (St. Martin's Press, 1989), pp. 101–102.

2 So called because it was paid for by the Pentagon's Advanced Research Projects Agency (ARPA).

3 Like many executives, Bob Lucky finds networks liberating.

> I inhabit a different social stratum on the computer networks than I do in real life. [In real life] I just can't walk down the aisles here and be an everyday person. They won't take me for that. In the computer network, there is very little social structure: there are only people and I know nothing about these people [whether they are] rich or poor or whatever.

4 C. Stoll, *The Cuckoo's Egg: Tracking a Spy through the Maze of Computer Espionage*, (Doubleday, 1989).

5 Contained in a draft letter from John Herschel to Henry Goulburn, Chancellor of the Exchequer, 1842, Royal Society Herschel Collection, box 27, item 51.

6 Good sources for details of software 'disasters' are Peter Neuman's 'Risks Forum' in *Communications of the ACM*. A recent book by Tom Forester and Perry Morrison, *Computer Ethics: Cautionary Tales and Ethical Dilemmas in Computing*, (MIT Press, 1990), has an excellent chapter 'Unreliable Computers' which has gathered together some of the most horrifying examples, some of which are included here.

7 In debates over whether software for the US strategic defence initiative (SDI) could be made reliable, AT&T was cited as proof that an extremely complex computer system could be made without flaws. See Peter G Neumann, 'Some reflections on a Telephone Switching Problem', *Communications of the ACM*, July 1990, vol. 33, No. 7, p. 154.

Further reading

General

A very good, detailed introduction to the history of computing until 1960 is Stan Augarten's *Bit by Bit: An Illustrated History of Computers* (Ticknor & Fields, 1984). For a pictorial history of early computing see Eames C & R, *A Computer Perspective* (Harvard University Press, 1973). A funny treatment is Larry Gonick's *The Cartoon Guide to Computer Science* (Barnes & Noble, 1983). The Time-Life Books *Understanding Computers Series* has two volumes *Computer Basics* and *Input/Output* with basic information. Also recommended is a special edition of the magazine *Computerworld* 'Celebrating the Computer Age: Man, Computers and Society', *Computerworld* 3 November 1986, which contains some illuminating interviews with pioneers.

Early computing

Good accounts of early computing are Michael R. Williams' *A History of Computing Technology* (Prentice-Hall,

Inc., 1985) and William Aspray's (Ed.) *Computing before Computers* (Iowa State Press, 1990). For the Second World War story the following are useful: Herman H. Goldstine's *The Computer from Pascal to von Neumann* (Princeton University Press, 1972); Metropolis, N. Howlett, J. and Gian-Carlo Rota *A History of Computing in the Twentieth Century* (Academic Press, 1980), and Nancy Stern's *From ENIAC to UNIVAC: An Appraisal of the Eckert-Mauchly Computers* (Digital Press, 1981). For the British scene see Maurice Wilkes' *Memoirs of a Computer Pioneer* (The MIT Press, 1985) and Simon Lavington's *Early British Computers* (Digital Press 1980).

Corporate Computing

A good account of the growth of the corporate computer industry is in Katharine Davis Fishman's *The Computer Establishment* (Harper & Row Publishers, 1981) (mainly about IBM) and David E. Lundstrom's *A Few*

Good Men from Univac (The MIT Press, 1987). See also: Regis McKenna's *Who's Afraid of Big Blue?* (Addison-Wesley Publishing Company, Inc., 1989); Peter Norton's *Inside the IBM PC* (Simon & Schuster, 1986); William W. Simmons' *Inside IBM: The Watson Years* (Dorrance and Company, Inc., 1988); Richard Thomas DeLamarter's *Big Blue: IBM's Use and Abuse of Power* (Dodd, Mead & Company, 1986); and Joel Shurkin's *Engines of the Mind; A History of the Computer* (W.W. Norton and Co., 1984).

The Silicon Revolution

For the microelectronic revolution see *Scientific American's Microelectronics* (W.H. Freeman & Co., 1977) and T.R. Reid's *Microchip: The Story of a Revolution and the Men who Made It* (William Collins & Sons Ltd., 1985). See also Dirk Hanson's *The New Alchemists: Silicon Valley and the Microelectronics Revolution* (Little, Brown & Co., 1982); Michael S. Malone's *The Big Score* (Doubleday and Co. Inc., 1985); and Everett M. Rogers and Judith K. Larsen's *Silicon Valley Fever* (Basic Books, Inc., Publisher, 1984).

The Personal Computer

For the rise of hobbyist computing and the Apple saga see Paul Freiberger and Michael Swaine's *Fire in the Valley: The Making of the Personal Computer* (Osbourne/McGraw-Hill, 1984); Frank Rose's *West of Eden: The End of Innocence at Apple Computer* (Viking Press, 1989); John Sculley's *Odyssey: Pepsi to Apple ...A Journey of Adventure, Ideas and the Future* (Harper & Row, 1987); and Jeffrey S. Young's *Steve Jobs: The Journey is the Reward* (Scott, Foresman and Co., 1988). For hackers and the computer counter-culture see Steven Levy's *Hackers: Heroes of the Computer Revolution* (Dell Publishing Company, 1984) and Ted Nelson's *Computer Lib: Dream Machines* (Tempus Books of Microsoft Press, 1974). For the dream of human-computer symbiosis from Licklider to Xerox PARC see Howard Rheingold's *Tools for Thought: The History and Future of Mind-Expanding Technology* (Simon & Schuster, 1985). Another software philosopher of interest is Fred Brooks. See Frederick P. Brooks' *The Mythical Man-month* (Addison-Wesley, 1982) and Ted Nelson's *Literary Machines*

(Swarthmore, PA 1987). For the Xerox PARC story see Douglas K. Smith and Robert C. Alexander's *Fumbling the Future: How Xerox Invented, then Ignored, the First Personal Computer* (William Morrow & Co., 1988).

Artificial intelligence

There is vast literature on Artificial Intelligence. This is a sample. Margaret A. Boden's *Artificial Intelligence and Natural Man* (Basic Books, Inc., Publishers, 1987); David J. Bolter's *Turing's Man: Western Culture in the Computer Age* (The University of North Carolina Press, 1984); Jeremy Campbell's *The Improbable Machine* (Simon & Schuster, 1989); Hubert L. Dreyfus' *What Computers Can't Do: The Limits of Artificial Intelligence* (Harper & Row, 1979); Hubert L. Dreyfus and Stuart E. Dreyfus' *Mind Over Machine: The Power of Human Intuition and Expertise in the Era of the Computer* (The Free Press, 1986); George Johnson's *Machinery of The Mind: Inside the New Science of Artificial Intelligence* (Times Books, 1986); Pamela McCorduck's *Machines Who Think* (W.H. Freeman and Company,

1977); Marvin Minsky's *The Society of Mind* (Simon & Schuster, 1985); Hans Moravec's *Mind Children: The Future of Robot and Human Intelligence* (Harvard University Press, 1988); F. David Peat's *Artificial Intelligence: How Machines Think* (Simon & Schuster, 1988); and Joseph Weizenbaum's *Computer Power and Human Reason: From Judgement to Calculation* (Pelican Books, 1976).

The connectionist vs. symbolic AI debate is played out in a special edition of the *Daedalus Journal of the American Academy of Arts and Sciences* 'Artificial Intelligence' (volume 117, Number 1, Winter 1988). Also see The DARPA Neural Network Study carried out by MIT's Lincoln Labs. For Alan Turing see Andrew Hodges' *Alan Turing: The Enigma* (Touchstone, Simon & Schuster, 1983). A useful insight into the state of the field in 1966 is given in Marvin Minsky's essay in *Scientific American's Information* (W.H. Freeman and Co., 1966).

Computer networking

For the social impact of computing and the issues surrounding computer

199

networking see Tom Forester's (Ed.) *Computers in the Human Context* (MIT Press, 1989); Tom Forester and Perry Morrison's *Computer Ethics: Cautionary Tales and Ethical Dilemmas in Computing* (MIT Press, 1990); George Gilder's *Microcosm: The Quantum Revolution in Economics and Technology* (Simon & Schuster, 1989); Clifford Stoll's *The Cuckoo's Egg: Tracking a Spy through the Maze of Computer Espionage* (Doubleday, 1989); Robert Lucky's *Silicon Dreams: Information, Man and Machine* (St Martin's Press, 1989) and Ithiel de Sola Pool's *Technologies of Freedom: On Free Speech in an Electronic Age* (Harvard University Press, 1983).

Glossary

Analog – continuously variable. A mercury thermometer is an example of an analog device: the column of mercury rises or falls smoothly as the temperature changes rather than changing in discrete jumps. In an analog device all the intermediate states are available and valid. Compare Digital.

Analog computer – a computer that operates with continuously variable quantities. Mechanical analog computers use the movement of spheres, discs and gearwheels, for example, to represent the quantities being calculated. Electronic analog computers use continuously variable electrical signals. The analog computer provides a model which follows the same rules that relate the quantities being computed. Compare Digital Computer.

Bit – short for 'binary digit'. A bit is the smallest unit of information in a binary number system. A bit in a computer can have only one of two values at any time. The value of a bit is usually referred to as '1' or '0'. Bit values are also referred to as 'hi' or 'lo', 'on' or 'off', and 'true' or 'false'.

Byte – a group of binary digits usually (but not necessarily) 8 bits long. In the most commonly used systems, one 8-bit byte is sufficient to represent one character such as a letter of the alphabet.

BASIC – acronym for Beginners All-purpose Symbolic Instruction Code. A comparatively simple programming language developed in the mid-1960s that beginners could learn quickly. BASIC allows the user to enter a list of instructions on a keyboard and run them directly (see INTERPRETER). Widely used by educational institutions, small businesses and hobbyists.

Capacitor – a device for storing an electrical charge. A common component in electrical and electronic circuits.

Cathode ray tube (CRT) – a device for displaying electrical signals visually. CRTs are used in radar displays, television and electronic measuring equipment. A beam of electrons is emitted from an electron 'gun' and accelerated towards a screen coated with a phosphor which glows when struck by electrons. The electron beam is deflected by the signals to be displayed and the trace produced on the screen follows the strength of the signal. The device is enclosed in a sealed funnel-shaped glass tube with a high vacuum inside.

Compiler – a computer program that translates a set of instructions written in a high-level language (FORTRAN, COBOL, for example) into a form that can be executed directly by the computer. It is much easier for programmers to write programs using high-level languages which allow statements that are closer to English commands than those required at machine level.

COBOL – acronym for Common Business-Oriented Language. A high-level programming language for commercial data processing. Became the most commonly used language for commercial applications after its introduction in 1960.

Diode – an electronic component that allows current to flow in one direction only. Since the 1960s diodes used in computer circuits are most commonly made from the semi-conducting material, silicon.

Disk drive – a device that can store and retrieve data on rotating magnetic discs. A floppy disk (so named because it is flexible) is an example of a removable magnetic disk that is placed in a disk drive. The disk drive can write information onto the disk and read data back from it.

Digital – using digits i.e. using discrete as opposed to continuous units. Compare Analog.

Digital computer – a computer that processes data digitally i.e. that operates on discrete quantities rather than continuous ones. Intermediate values between the allowed counting units are not recognized. Compare Analog computer.

FORTRAN – acronym for FORmula TRANslation. A high-level programming language issued in 1957 widely used for scientific computation.

Hardware – the physical parts of a computer system. These include circuit components, disk drives, terminals and cabinets. Compare Software.

Integrated circuit (IC) – a small piece of semiconductor material fabricated to include a complete electronic circuit (mostly diodes and transistors) as an integral part of its structure. The 'chip' of semiconductor material (most commonly silicon) is sealed in a package (usually plastic). 'IC' and 'chip' are often used interchangeably to refer to the piece of fabricated silicon with or without its package.

Interpreter – a computer program that analyzes an instruction written in one language and carries out the required actions directly. In BASIC, for example, the translation is usually done line-by-line. Compare Compiler.

Interactive computing – used to describe a mode of working in which users secure a response to their input as it occurs. Sometimes called conversational mode. This is in contrast to 'off line' working where the programs and data are prepared on a separate station and input to the computer on cards, tape or disk. In 'off line' working there is a delay between the input and the response.

Kilobyte – one thousand bytes (strictly 2^{10} bytes i.e. 1024 bytes). (See Byte).

Logic gate – a device that implements an elementary logical operation. Examples include gates for AND, NAND, OR, NOR and NOT functions. The output of any gate is determined by the logical states of its inputs. The output of an AND gate, for example, will only be 'true' ('1') if *all* its inputs are 'true'. The output of an OR gate will be 'true' if any of its inputs are 'true'. A NOT gate will invert its input to produce a '1' at the output if the input is '0', and a '0' at the output if the input is '1'. Logic gates need not be electronic. There are mechanical and electromechanical versions of these logic functions.

203

Megabyte – a million bytes. (See Byte).

Mercury delay line – a computer memory device for storing electronic pulses. Developed in the 1940s. Uses the principle that sound waves travel more slowly than electrical signals. Electrical pulses were converted into sound waves and sent down a column of mercury. The time taken to reach the end of the column provides the delay. To store the pulses they were kept circulating continuously round the tube by detecting them at the receiving end and feeding them back to the input via circuits that corrected any deterioration. In computing, acoustic delay lines of this kind are now of historical interest only.

Microprocessor – a semi conductor chip that contains the central processor of a computer. The first commercially available microprocessor was the INTEL 4004 in 1971.

Resistor – an electrical component that impedes the flow of electric current in a circuit.

Relays – electromechanical switching devices extensively used in pre-electronic telephone exchanges.

Software – the programs executed by a computer system as distinct from the physical hardware (see Hardware). Used to refer to intangible rather than physical components of a computer system.

Stereo head-up display – a head-up display is a term used in avionics to describe a method of display that allows a pilot to see information produced by instruments while still looking ahead. The images are superimposed by projection on the view through the windscreen. In the context of virtual worlds a head-up display refers to a helmet worn by the user. The helmet has a tracking system that informs the controlling computer of its position and of the direction of gaze. The computer produces images in the eyepieces, which correspond to movements of the user's head. The display is called 'stereo' because the computer generates separate images for each eye to create the illusion of depth. The computer adjusts the images as the user moves and the system creates the illusion of being immersed in a three dimensional world.

Tape drive – device for storing and retrieving information on reels of magnetic tape. The data is written and read serially i.e. as a long string.

Valve/vacuum tube – devices first used in radio and radar circuits for detecting, amplifying and processing electrical signals. Consist of a sealed tubular glass envelope with metal plates inside which control the movement of electrons emitted from a heated filament. Used as electronic switches in the first electronic computers in the 1940s. Began to be replaced by transistors in the late 1950s. In England referred to as thermionic valves or simply valves. In the United States the same devices are called vacuum tubes.

205

*I*ndex